Dream
pools & gardens

Dream

pools & gardens

By Francisco Asensio Cerver

Stewart, Tabori & Chang
NEW YORK

Author   Francisco Asensio Cerver

Editorial director Jordi Vigué

Graphic designer   Mireia Casanovas Soley

Layout designer   Jaume Martínez Coscojuela

Translator & Proofreader   Harry Paul

Photographers   © Melba Levick (p. 26, 82, 86, 90, 94, 180)

© Eugeni Pons/Piscines Costa Brava (p. 6, 10, 12, 18, 46, 56, 70,
76, 80, 124, 128, 134, 140, 144, 150, 152, 156, 158, 168)

© Guillaume de Laubier (p. 38, 50, 52, 54, 104, 108, 112, 116, 196, 200, 202)

© Pere Planells (p. 30, 34, 42, 62, 66, 68, 98, 102, 118, 130, 160, 164,
174, 176, 182, 186, 190, 194, 206)

© Mihail Moldoveavu (p. 58, 72)

© Joan Mundó (p. 120)

© Jordi Sarrà (p. 8, 20)

© Dominique Delaunay (p. 14)

Stylists   Elena Calderon (*Comfort and aesthetics*; *Like a boat*,
Less is more)

Angels G.Giró (*The last afternoon hour*; *An idyllic landscape*)

Published in 1999 by
Stewart, Tabori & Chang
A division of U.S. Media Holdings, Inc.
115 West 18th Street
New York, NY 10011

Distributed in Canada by
General Publishing Company Ltd.
30 Lesmill Road
Don Mills, Ontario, Canada M3B 2T6

Asensio Cerver, Francisco.
[Piscinas de ensueño. English]
Dream pools & gardens / Francisco Asensio Cerver.
p.   cm.
ISBN 1-55670-907-2 (alk. paper)
1. Swimming pools. 2. Gardens. I. Title.
TH4763.A84   1999
728'.962--dc21   99-10489
CIP

Design by Arco Editorial Graphic Studio
Printed in Spain

10 9 8 7 6 5 4 3 2 1
First Printing

Introduction   6

Panoramic swimming pools   8
Among the trees   10
The open sky   12
Bathing in the mountains   14
Two levels   18
A framed landscape   20
The path of water   26
Comfort and aesthetics   30
The garden with different atmospheres   34
The beauty of the horizon   38
Respecting the past   42
Three different atmospheres   46
A picturesque landscape   50
Light and shadow   52
A season in the country   54

Architectural swimming pools   56
Symmetry and reflection   58
By the wall   62
Between the porch and the garden   66
The garden and the city   68
The inside circle   70
Right next to the living room   72
A privileged position   76
Keep in shape   80
An intimate garden   82
The domestic oasis   86
An Asian touch   90
From the pool   94
Between two butresses   98
Near and comfortable   102
What summer means   104
White atop green   108

Extending the living room   112
Around the water's edge   116
Harmony and health   118
The reflection of the architecture   120
A double curve   124

Mediterranean swimming pools   128
Like a boat   130
The double line on the horizon   134
Going to the edge   138
Between the sea and the sky   140
When night falls   144
Beautiful and easy to use   146
A style exercise   150
A waterfall   152
A simple garden   156
Visual continuity   158
Less is more   160
A well-deserved rest   164
A swimming pool with a view   168
A water canal   170

Tropical swimming pools   174
Backlight   176
A tradition of comfort   180
The last afternoon hour   182
A space to be shared   186
An idyllic landscape   190
Natural scenery   194
Luxury and comfort   196
A light spot   200
One's own territory   202
Blending in with the landscape   206

Architectural beauty is enigmatic. Creating it takes more than good intentions. Neither the finest materials nor the most advanced technology guarantee its achievement in the same way that a literary masterpiece does not depend on top-quality ink. According to Adolf Loos, in all of architecture only a small part belongs to art: the tomb and the monument. Everything else, everything that has a purpose, must be excluded from what is art. It is true that practically all architectural constructions do have a function, but there are some that straddle the fine dividing line between what is functional and what is purely aesthetic.

This book presents a series of swimming pools that flirt with that fragile frontier of beauty and utilitarianism. They are swimming pools that fuse these two ways of approaching architecture, with one of them superceding the other in each different case. The four sections have been arranged according to three criteria: geographical location, climate (tropical pools and Mediterranean pools), and the similarities between the way in which the projects were conceived (pools integrated into the architecture and panoramic pools).

PANORAMIC
SWIMMING POOLS

In this section the projects that have given priority to the environment in which they are placed have been grouped together. To be more precise, the pools are situated where it is easiest to take advantage of the natural features of the landscape and to absorb the ambience that surrounds them, and where the view stretches to the horizon. They are like animals that lie on the ground after having looked around for the best spot from which to watch out over the territory and enjoy the view that nature offers. These pools give character to a landscape that calls out to be contemplated. The contemporary home builder constructs these pools as lookout points that reveal the size of humankind—very small, indeed, compared to the vastness of nature. Humankind redefines its status and reconsiders its scale of values, which has been so corrupted by daily life.

On the following pages you will see swimming pools from Spain, the Balearic Islands, Switzerland, California, Greece, the Azores Islands, and the French Riviera.

Among the trees

Cala Montgoda. Spain

With its softly curved shape, the swimming pool blends in perfectly with the garden.

The pool is at the optimal distance from the house.

Choosing the shape, size, and placement of the swimming pool is crucial when it comes to designing a garden. If the pool is near the house, straight lines and rectangles make the most of the available space. If it is further away, a soft, curved profile that can be adapted to the irregular features of the landscape and reduces the intensity of the land contours is the goal. The starkness of an angular perimeter is thereby eliminated.

The grand house looms over the space. The entrance area is extended by a terrace that overlooks the pool. It is invigorating to lean on the iron railing first thing in the August morning to watch the forest wake up in the heat, to listen to the insects and cicadas buzzing, and to smell the Mediterranean grass. There is also a terrace on the ground floor: The house is staggered until it reaches the grass and tree level. Next to the wall and in front of the swimming pool there is a little garden in which flowers, tiny palm trees, and diverse plants grow among the rocks.

The terrace protrudes a little, offering some shade where a bar has been set up. After a swim, feeling the heat of the sun, we can lounge on a stool and enjoy some refreshment in the shade. Everything is so well planned that even the wall has a small ridge that is used as a bottle shelf. This amusing, insignificant detail imparts an incongruent, almost whimsical touch to this rustic atmosphere.

The large grass lawn is bathed in sunlight all day. There is only one shade tree to cool things down along one side, where we can lie down on the grass without a towel to feel the soft sweet-smelling ground beneath us. The double curve of the swimming pool is delineated by a rim in prestressed concrete, whose clear tone gives the impression of a line that separates the water plane from the green grass. All these features add up to form a pleasant place to swim in the heart of the forest.

The swimming pool bottom has been covered with irregular stones, the cracks between which make it look like a country pavement.

The swimming area is at the optimal distance from the house: near enough to be comfortably reached when carrying clothes and other items from the house, and far enough to ensure privacy and peace when swimming.

The open sky

Colera. Spain

The large scale of the swimming pool fits the vast expanse of the landscape.

The great mass of rock leads down to the sea. The coast is precipitous and arduous to reach.

This swimming pool is situated on a flat, spacious plot overlooking a mountainous landscape with the sea in the foreground. If we turn off the highway a group of houses that share a common esplanade come into view. In one corner lies the swimming pool, just before the ground gives way to the slope. Around the pool there is a treeless lawn that increases the sensation of freedom of movement that we had when we first drove in. Horizontal lines dominate a landscape in which the human figure serves to emphasize the grand scale of its true dimensions.

The house has an ample terrace overlooking the sea and pool. When the sun is high, the water planes glisten. On the first floor the terrace is the structure that shades the entrance.

The land is sparsely populated: There is a palpable sensation of withdrawal and liberty. The coastline is quite abrupt, the vegetation is low, and the pines have adapted to the slope. In summer the still seawater darkens the shoreline rocks and reflects the shape of the mountain. The sea is difficult to reach even in a four-wheel-drive vehicle. Indeed part of the charm of the landscape has been conserved thanks to this inaccessibility. In the final stretch the path becomes overgrown and swimmers must forge their own path, stumbling over the boulders until they reach the water. There is no sandy beach here, but rather a cozy cove. If we are relaxed and do not feel like rambling down to the sea, we can do some strokes up in the pool, glancing occasionally at the blue horizon.

This swimming pool area has no flowers or foliage. There is no protection from the sun, no shady corners: The exposition is total. In the air there hangs a feeling of desolation, of bareness, which perhaps is due to the fact that the project is not totally finished.

Bathing in the mountains

Philippe Rothier Residence
Ibiza. Spain

The inhabitants of a rural dwelling in the midst of the mountains know how to economize their efforts to get the most out of their resources. The term "to waste" does not make much sense in this situation. Materials are recycled, buildings are reconverted, and maximum use is obtained from everything. Novelty consists in precisely this.

This pool in the middle of these backwoods has been built out of an abandoned water deposit that rises out of the ground. On top of the walls prestressed concrete has been used to construct a rim from which to dive, or you can lie down by the water's edge to bask in the sun.

The old deposit seems like a volume that has come to rest here by chance. Its layout is vaguely reminiscent of a primitive Roman church where the greenery has grown unrestrained over the walls as if it wanted to creep into the water. It is a typically Mediterranean forest, with holm oaks, pines, prickly pears, shrubs with thorny branches, and a dry aromatic soil.

If we stand under the wooden beamed porch we can look out over the valley. There are no neatly laid-out crop fields. We are in the middle of a forest whose beauty is the shady stillness under the branches.

The swimming pool rises out of the ground with its solid walls.

From the porch there is
a fine view over the
whole valley. The pool
is in the foreground.

In rural architecture it is common for new buildings to be added on gradually, as the owners' needs evolve and the families grow. This is why the shapes are often heterogeneous and integrated into the topography in different ways. The windows are narrow to protect the inside from the unrelenting sun. The small rooms have thick load walls and high ceilings crossed by irregular beams. Walking from one room to another,

one notices that rooms have been added on in a hodgepodge manner: They have different atmospheres and are isolated from each other. However, the feeling of distance between the rooms is even greater than the reality.

Just as each room is individual, in the same way the swimming pool appears as an island amid the vegetation. Each element carries out its specific function.

The angles of the
swimming pool recall the
rocks around the edge.

Two levels

The best way to take advantage of a sloping piece of ground is to form terraces as the farmers do. In the case of building a house, this problem can be solved in the same way, only we enter on one level and then ascend to the lower one. When the swimming pool is constructed it is necessary to bear in mind with which area of the house it is going to be related. Here it has been placed in the upper part of the garden, which is joined to a terrace marked off with geometric flowerpots. From this vantage point there are magnificent panoramic views down the hillside, with treetops silhouetted against the sky.

The swimming pool outline has sharp edges like the rocks around it, a feature that helps it blend in with the grounds. Like the house, the pool is divided into two levels. Above there is a water plane that extends as far as the edge of the slope over which it flows; a few yards below, another pool fragment collects the waterfall.

A landscape in which the tones and shades of green predominate is enhanced by this bluish spark of color among the trees.

If the top of the swimming pool is at ground level and the water next to the grass, the small lower pool is like a container: Its walls come out of the ground. Aesthetics have priority over function on the upper level, while it is clear that the small pool below is designed to collect the falling water.

Gardens and houses in Mediterranean climates suffer from a shortage of water in summer. Sometimes it does not rain for two months or more, and therefore a watering system is vital to keep everything green. Often if the land is near the sea the salinity of the water is harmful to the plants. We must bear these factors in mind when we choose the species that will compose the garden.

A framed landscape

Architect: Javier de Olaso
Ibiza. Spain

The architecture of the arches is superceded by the horizontal lines of the swimming pool.

A dream is the force behind creativity. Dreaming is a healthy break, a source of inspiration and ideas, a time when forms and shapes come to mind. Bathing in one's own swimming pool is a dream that can be realized. A pool is a symbol of well-being, affluence, leisure, health, and hedonism.

Water lends itself to playful social activities. For a long time bathing in the open air, lying in the sun, and watersports were the pursuits only of the upper or wealthy classes. Nowadays this custom is firmly implanted in all levels of society. The beaches and the pools have been demonstrably democratized.

A swimming pool is always something creative. To conceive it and to draw it are, in some way, a means of jumping into it. The simplest rectangular container can become an original and creative project thanks to the materials used to build it, the way it is designed to fit into the environment, and the colors or the finishing details and trimmings used to embellish it.

Vertical-line architecture can be rediscovered thanks to the water plane, which acts as a mirror. This effect, which is commonly used in swimming pools filled to the limit, owes a lot to the architectural tradition that seeks to exploit the fact that the real and virtual image are so complementary. According to Islamic culture, reflections had a symbolic value and evoked "the delights of Paradise."

This swimming pool was designed with an unusual lookout point in mind. The sea- and pool-water surfaces harmonize to form one continuous line as a result of the visual superimposition of the two planes. It seems as if you can reach out and touch the sea from the terrace. The foreground of the "set" takes on a sculptured and dramatic look as it is silhouetted against a clean background. Placing the water plane at the top of the slope means that any buildings that may be below do not spoil the sight.

Choosing the rim material that will frame the swimming pool is an important aesthetic and technical question. With this pool the pavement goes to the edge of the water, and therefore the final slabs must be thicker to act both as a pavement and as a rim.

If you want to create a rich color contrast between the sea color and the pool water the finishing color of the pool materials must be chosen accordingly. If it has smooth texture and a light tone the swimming pool will have a tropical beach shoreline color, typical of the bright sands and the almost transparent turquoise of the sea. In the background dark blue will finish off the picture.

Protected by the loggia of the house, we can enjoy some magnificent views.

The path of water

Hugh Heffner Residence
Beverly Hills. California. USA

The water runs over the rocks, leading us to discover new hidden corners.

If travel photography had not developed in the second half of the nineteenth century many foreign countries and their cultural heritage would have remained unknown to a great part of the population who were not well off enough to go abroad. This is how photography brought exotic landscapes and different cultures, which today are sources of much artistic inspiration, nearer.

Architecture was influenced by distant cultures and incorporated new images. Romanticism, with its love of the old legends, was the forerunner of today's world, which delights in the natural outdoor life and sport. Landscapist techniques aim at re-creating spaces in which it is difficult to notice human intervention, where nature imposes its own law free from the restraints of order and symmetry.

This pool has been designed in an effort to create a natural effect, following the natural course of the water tumbling over the rocks and waterfalls amid the plentiful greenery. The classical architects mastered the art of creating a waterfall, or a bank, while respecting the rock geometry. Here something similar has been attempted. From the very start it is imperative to be clear about what type of ambience you seek. Mixing areas exposed to the sun for long hours alternatively with shady and intimate corners yields good results, as do interludes when the water calms down and silence reigns contrasted with noisy splashes giving off beams of light. Smells and vegetation are other ingredients in the landscaper's palette that reinforce the wild, natural aspect of the rocks.

When a natural swimming pool is conceived, it is as important to consider the form as it is to study the plant and tree composition. Bushes or fruit trees, deciduous leaf, or resinous needle-leaf trees have deliberately not been planted near the water. Hydrophilic plants have roots that grow out, invading all that lies in their path. The greenery has been carefully chosen to set the right scene.

Trees can give rise to special problems, for their roots can even break or crack the swimming pool walls or interfere with the underground water pipes. One solution is to channel the roots downward by using a system of three or four plastic tubes that are buried around the tree, forming a circle. They must be about four inches long and four inches in diameter. The base is perforated so that the water can filter through. The trees are regularly watered by pouring water into these tubes and thus saturating the soil at this depth with water, inducing the roots to shoot downward.

Comfort and aesthetics

Designer: Ricardo Urgell
Ibiza. Spain

The lawn runs up to
the very poolside.

Amid a thickly wooded forest whitewashed walls come into view. They belong to a two-story house with a magnificent garden and luminous lawn. Galleries and porches finish off this unobtrusive dwelling.

If we are high up on the terrace we can contemplate the beauty of the landscape as it gently slopes away from us. A mountain range is cut out in the background, while the swimming pool occupies the foreground. The pool imitates the gentle curve of a pond. The edge is totally covered by grass so that it seems that it is in contact with the water, thus increasing the illusion of it being a natural reservoir. Only upon entering into the water do we discover the brick confines. The image somewhat resembles some Nordic beaches where the hillsides run down to the open sea.

For many years city dwellers have sought places to escape from the bustle landscapes that enable the constant to-and-fro of downtown to be forgotten, silent spaces in which to leave the office behind. Nature offers us this soothing calmness, prompting us to look for an isolated house on its own grounds where we can create an artificial paradise. We will have two lives: stress on weekdays and tranquillity on weekends. The drawback is sometimes the distance of these second residences, which leads to the freeway traffic jams as everybody heads out of the cities on Friday evening.

In the middle of the lawn we can stretch out on the deck chairs to sunbathe. If the heat is oppressive, the best solution is to take a dip or to retreat to a shady corner where there is a sofa with cushions. The materials used both for the architecture and the furniture are natural and rustic. Glass and metal only appear as secondary actors. The dark woodwork contrasts with the light walls.

Each corner has been thought out, giving priority to comfort and aesthetics. The family has to get the most out of the free time they have worked so hard to achieve.

There are corners to rest in, islands
of silence where you can unwind.

33

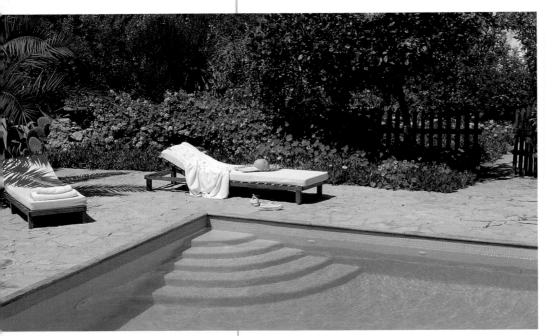

The garden
with different
atmospheres

Designer: Françoise Pialoux
Ibiza. Spain

At one end of the pool, in the corners, some circular stairs gently lead down into the water.

When the first hot days begin to arrive the house opens up. The fresh air starts to penetrate a space that has been closed up during the winter. The summer light illuminates daily life, which as the days go by takes place outside more and more.

It is time to tidy up the garden so that we can enjoy it during the sunny season. The architectural elements and the landscape can be combined if the communication between them is interpreted correctly. Stairs, pergolas, stone or whitewashed walls, pavements, embankments, flower beds, plants, and lawns all add to the effect around the pool.

There are many variables the architect can play with, and the potential results are infinite. All that is necessary is to be clear about the particular ambience we want to create. A medium, family-sized swimming pool presides over the garden. Around the clear, blue, shimmering pool there is a stone pavement on which to sunbathe. Beyond this the greenery comes into its own, marking the boundaries between the different areas and softening the heat. On one side, a little bit above ground level, stands a table for open-air meals. The access to this area is through a somewhat vague plant arch—plants give each area its own personality.

Besides the overall effect that is at the forefront of the designer's mind, the garden also needs many little details. For example, the idea of conserving rather constructing requires sensibility to retouch, adapt, enlarge, complete, and continue what already exists. A love of small points, not born of theory or study, is necessary. In architecture the material realization of a project can never be considered separately from its conception; they condition each other. The same wall, plastered or covered in stone, can take on a radically different look.

The garden is characterized by different corners that have been designed for intimate social gatherings.

In the foreground of the expansive landscape, the wicker chairs appear as fragile objects.

The beauty of the horizon

Pringle. Portugal

Introducing a swimming pool into the house where you go to get away from it all opens up a range of possibilities for leisure and sport, and has proved to be a home improvement hit. This custom started out with the acquisition of summer residences but it quickly spread, and nowadays it is difficult to find weekend retreats, apartments, or hotels that do not have their own pool. However, this is a recent phenomenon which caught on surprisingly quickly. A 1921 dictionary did not include the term "swimming pool" as we understand it. A smile creeps across our faces when we read this definition: "Swimming pool: a pond in the garden which normally contains fish."

There is an abyss between this concept and the swimming pool that we can see in the photos, not just in time but also in the social aspect and attitude. This pool has been approached as a meeting point, the focus of social relations. Instead of chatting around a table, we do it poolside. Bathing and swimming are shared activities, to play and to get fit. The classic tradition of the spas and public baths has been re-created, but the context has been changed. Before pools became popular the architect designed an interior, but here we have gone outside to enjoy direct contact with nature. Right angles and symmetry are replaced by soft forms and pure lines analogous to natural growth. The surrounding landscape seems to have been flattened by the wind, as if everything has to be at ground level. Likewise the architecture is adapted to the land: It does not dominate. Its horizontality prevails. The structures are spread out and grouped like the vegetation in the area.

Canvas deck chairs have been spread around the pool for sunbathing. The furniture and fixtures have to be included in the design project; materials and forms must harmonize.

This project has used few decorative elements; however, the resulting spaces are cozy, neat, and warm. Today ornaments are not a synonym for luxury and comfort, or aesthetics. In architecture uncluttered spaces and simplicity are at a premium.

The circular form of the swimming
pool fosters social interaction.

From this perspective we can appreciate three very different textures: stone, flowers, and water.

Respecting the past

Designer: Mary Cantarell
Girona. Spain

I n the creator's mind, past, present, and future play a role as he or she conceptualizes the design; otherwise his or her inventions would soon fade away with time.

Over thousands of years humankind has been evolving physically to adapt to the world. The faculty to create has remained unchanged in this time; only the environment has changed—radically. Society sees change as something positive and some architects are seriously committed to it.

This could be related to our tendency to draw a line between the past and the future, producing a strange emotional relationship with the present. The present is soon "heard no more." We must not be sentimental or get too bogged down in the past. Neither should we let the future become too technological. We must begin with the past so that we can discover what is immutable in humankind.

When a new element is built in an already established context—in this case rural—tradition must be respected but without totally submitting to the norms of the past. We can introduce a new language or different materials that bring forth a positive contrast. However, it is always a delicate balance. On the subject of a building by the side of a lake, the Austrian architect Adolf Loos asked, "But what is this? A note out of tune with the harmony. Like an uncalled for shout. In the center, below the farmworkers' houses, which were not created by them but by God, a villa appears. Is it the product of a skilled or clumsy architect? I don't know. I only know that peace, tranquillity and beauty no longer exist. And let me ask another question: Why does the architect, regardless of whether he or she is skilled or clumsy, violate the lake? Like nearly all the city dwellers architects don't have a natural culture. They do not have the same makeup as the country person for whom this culture is innate. The city dweller is a newcomer, an upstart."

Culture is that equilibrium of humankind between the internal and the external. Culture guarantees that rational thought and action are possible. This project is steeped in the harmony between the past and the current language. The noble

Behind the wall the holm oak and pine spread out, forming a dark green background that fills the stone foreground with color.

materials, like rock and wood, are discretely used in order to favor the integration of the architecture with the landscape. The swimming pool is extended along the wall and building line. The slabs around the swimming pool are packed together and prevent the gravel in the garden from getting into the pool. The transparency of the water reflects the flowers next to the wall, adding color to the scene.

The furnishings are perfectly integrated into the design of the swimming pool.

Three different atmospheres

Santorini. Greece

Swimming pools can be just water containers or they can incorporate into their design equipment that offers their users extra comforts. Here the outline of the swimming pool changes as new elements are introduced. Some steps run down until they are covered by water, and the deck chairs aligned along the edge introduce a color contrast.

In this pool there are two atmospheres separated by a wall that juts out of the water slightly. First sit down on the gently descending steps and then enjoy a leisurely swim. The transition from rest to exercise can be gradual rather than brusque. This area relieves stress and invites you to converse and soak up the tranquillity, like in the old baths or spas, whose atmosphere put their guests at ease in a way different from that of the squares or cafés. The context helped the conversation. Nowadays people go to swimming pools to have a good time. The standard rectangular swimming pool can be imaginatively turned into a host of different forms.

In the other part of the swimming pool there are aquatic flowerpots containing plants which mark the path down the stairs into the water. The deck chairs are shielded from the people coming and going. At the other end is the swimming area, which is deeper and therefore allows the diving board to be used without risk. This pool plays with the longitudinal symmetry. At night a lighting system converts the water into the center of attention, enticing people to use the garden.

"Summer" is a synonym for "relaxation" and "tranquillity," but it is also a time to make new resolutions, like for example doing away with a sedentary life that working in a city imposes on us and starting to engage in a sport. Swimming is one of the most often recommended sports for muscles that have not been put through their paces for a long time, for the movements are soft and harmonious and one can stretch to one's limit without doing any harm. Crawl or breast stroke exercises the whole body. We feel lighter in the water and our movements are less abrupt. Moreover, in summer this sport

takes us out into the open air where we are surrounded by a lush garden.

When designing a swimming pool we have to think about the different atmospheres that will coexist. The various spaces that each activity will require are drawn out. We make sure that they are compatible, for this mixture will enhance and enrich the architecture. The pool and garden have to reflect the complexity of the varied ambiences; they do not exist in isolation.

The symmetry is the dominant note in
the composition of this project.

The white paint on the trees introduces a surreal element into the landscape.

A picturesque landscape

St. Tropez. France

The word "garden" is masculine in Spanish, French, and German. However, in all these languages it is associated with femininity. The garden is the ground that contains the plants and receives the seeds and the fertilizer for the soil. The *fin-de-siècle* writers tirelessly described the gardens that provided the ideal setting for falling in love and thus established them as a literary topic. Gardens contain century-old trees, labyrinthine paths, and fences or hedges. Gardens also have a symbolic value. Normally it is here that love scenes take place against the backdrop of tamed nature, the sensuality of which reinforces the passion.

A garden also transmits the sensation of harmony that music and poetry offer. The proportions of this garden, its open spaces, and its hideaways give it rhythm. However, added to the historic approach there is an element that transforms it and allows art to participate in nature. The trees that line the large avenue have been painted white up to a certain height. Such an obvious manipulation introduces an element of surprise which catches the eye of the passer-by.

The swimming pool is situated on the upper plane, on the same level as the treetops in the walkway. The swimming pool is a neoplasticist plane: the linear relations are restricted to vertical and horizontal movements. It is one color, a geometric form implanted in a classical landscape. The large slab pavement reaches to the water's edge, where bushes and deck chairs have been situated to contemplate the panorama.

Humans can leave their mark on nature in many ways: An interstate freeway cutting geometrically through a wood is one example. Or it can be the shape of a tree after pruning, as we can see in the cypresses in the labyrinth. Wherever men and women go they leave their stamp branded, sometimes to good effect, as in this case, and sometimes to ill, muddling up the environment thoughtlessly.

The line of the swimming pool outlines the treetops. In the background the blue waves gently glisten.

Painting the trees could be regarded as artistic. The vanguard movements, painting and art in general, are now less concerned with representing "what's out there"; instead the support (the "canvas"), the techniques, and the limitations have become part of the expression. This is the moment when art, understood in the traditional sense, dies and gives way to vanguardism. With this garden the normal support for painting, the "canvas," is replaced by nature itself: the tree trunks are part of the representation. The landscape is not depicted according to the standard conventions; it is a work of art on its own.

Light and shadow

When there is a lot of free land around the house, even with forests and a garden, the placement of the swimming pool is straightforward. A garden area can be designed specifically to accommodate the pool, choosing everything appropriately: its size, the materials, the plants, and the furniture. Having a lot of liberty does not take away the need to remember certain practical criteria. There are advantages in placing it near the house but it must be protected from intrusive views by the entrance. Around the house there is a forest of luxuriant trees offering an ideal shady place in which to stroll in summer. To cool down we can dive into the pool and then stretch out on the deck chairs, enjoying nature. A cozy atmosphere must be created both in the garden and in the house. Good ideas and taste come into play when laying out the plants and vegetation. Consulting a horticulturalist or a landscaper is never a bad idea. Just as an architect is entrusted with the house project, so too a wise person can advise us about the garden.

Strolling tranquilly through the clearing around the pool we can appreciate the color composition of the house, the annexes, and the landscape. The materials are harmonious because they are noble and from nearby. The stone, the wood, and the ceramics have been treated according to traditional building methods.

In this garden it is the house that imposes itself because of its location and the fact that the majority of the paths lead to it. There is a certain Italian influence as well as a nuance of the romantic. The central avenue is softened by the plants and trees along the side, which results in a zigzagging perspective rather than a straight line. Sometimes we come into little clearings where the sun enters, or shadier areas.

These lush gardens, which have only acquired their full splendor after many years, are the ideal assurance of our privacy. This space is a microcosm in which to disconnect from the asphalt jungle, a green belt around the house that acts as a visual and acoustic barrier.

The pool, with its own sunbathed lawn, is next to the forest.

Together the shady and dark corners make up a varied garden.

A season in the country

Provence. France

The house is surrounded by a large gardened area. This enables the swimming pool to be fair sized.

The rim is eight inches above the level of the grass so that neither leaves nor soil fall into the water.

Away from the densely populated big-city sprawls, we can find the tranquillity we deserve and need. As we approach the country, trees, flowers, and plants start to appear. The scents in the air begin to change. A world that we thought had disappeared comes to life before us, reminding us that we were born to be in contact with nature.

The distances are much greater in the country. Proximity takes on a new meaning. The houses outside the city limits have land around them like a barrier. In the old days this land was often a vegetable plot, or a garden to work in. Then it was inconceivable for there to be a home without its own landscape around it. To be a landowner was the ultimate aspiration in bygone days.

Over the years these properties have changed hands continuously, and have often been subdivided. They have ceased to be economic units that exist to make a profit: People no longer work in them. Animals are not reared, nor are crops grown. They are now places dedicated to relaxing and having a good time during vacations. The mind can wind down and let off steam; our heavy thoughts can float among the green spaces. At last we have escaped from the pollution and the noise. Instead of fumes and asphalt we can look over a lawn that only ends when it abuts the trees planted by our ancestors—or by the old owners. The swimming pool, in the middle of this mellow scene, is a plane of water, like a mirror. Near the pool there are no trees so that the sun heats up the water and we can sunbathe. The edge of the pool is slightly elevated to give it a more rustic, less sophisticated air. The water is kept clean: Neither leaves nor grass are allowed to fall in because of the high ledge.

When we spend more time outdoors, it is invigorating to find nooks and recesses where the light is filtered by the greenery. On the main façade of many country houses a vine has grown up around the entrance. It is a kind of protection for it can sometimes form a small archlike structure. Sometimes it need not even be a vine but some other type of creeper. In other areas, a light structure that forms a pergola is the ideal setting for a big celebration.

ARCHITECTURAL SWIMMING POOLS

The swimming pools that are presented on the following pages have in common the fact that they form part of a project that includes other constructions that are part of the house. Sometimes the pools are indoors, but they can also be outside. In either case, they always reflect the same construction criteria as those used to build the house. This means that they are in synch with the global project, for they are the fruit of a unique architectural approach that has not made qualitative distinctions between the garden and the house.

There are some examples in which it is the pool itself that mitigates the frontier between inside and outside. The pool is the medium that takes us out of the house into the garden. It is an element of transition between the architecture and the landscape.

With these projects we will visit examples from Barcelona, Ibiza, Lleida, and the Costa Brava in Spain; Rimini and Tuscany in Italy; Axel Verwoot in Belgium; Miami, Los Angeles, Palm Springs, and San Francisco in the United States; Corsica and Provence in France; Sydney in Australia and Dominican Republic.

Symmetry and reflection

Architect: Oscar Tusquets
Barcelona. Spain

The arrangement of the planes of water gives strength to the symmetry of the residential project as a whole. The reflections multiply and enrich the architecture.

This pool, a mixture of canal and pond, is situated in the residence of Oscar Tusquets. It is a glowing example of how to take advantage of water for architectural benefit. The swimming pool is an extension of the style of the house as it echoes the Islamic tradition of using different water planes. The water is contained within architectural elements that play with the symmetry proposed by the house, sometimes reflecting it and sometimes breaking it.

In both cases the water is used in an almost abstract manner, as if it were another building material. The swimming pool is sometimes a canal, at other times a pond, but it is always organizing the space around the house. The walls that form the canal serve as benches as well as parterres for flowers.

The color contrast between the materials of the house and those of the garden create a strange effect. On the façade the clarity and purity of the lines are dominant: The elements are framed in white. In the garden the concrete reconciles the architecture with the earth: The water becomes darker and the vegetation creates shady areas.

This swimming pool, in contrast to the house, which is perceived as a compact and single entity, is fragmented into different forms and diverse locations. This encourages the visitor to take a walk around, changing the perspective.

The different levels of the water create a complex and rich environment that constructs a personal garden around the house. As in Islamic palaces the water layout adds character to the patios. The spaces are open and everything can be observed from a high vantage point.

In this project, Tusquets has combined perfectly elements of modern architecture with a language that expresses the tradition of the classic villas.

The water is held back by walls that form canals. The water practically overflows and appears as an almost abstract horizontal plane.

These walls serve as parterres planted with trees and vegetation as well as benches to sit on.

Water is another architectural
element, acting as a mirror
creating a new landscape.

The architect has played
with the layout of the
garden, arranging it on
different levels so that
some areas are cozy and
shielded from prying views.

By the wall

Designer: Lola de Quinto
Ibiza. Spain

The terrace-garden has been paved with a spongy porous rock. Around the trees and tall vegetation there are parterres that have not been paved over. The vegetation consists of olive and palm trees, and aromatic grasses. The vegetation is framed by a pergola with stone columns and covered by wooden beams on which the vine has started to twist round, creating a shady zone.

S ituated on a headland in front of the sea, the town masks the profile of the slope with its large stone wall, its gardens, and its double-sided roofs. The different levels create intermediate spaces that have been turned into terraces that offer marvelous views. Sometimes these terraces, which have been designated as viewing areas, are at ground level, where the streets widen. In other places these terraces are in private gardens that are reached by going up or down stairs. These architectural gardens, so well integrated into the urban layout, are perfectly marked off. Their combinations of rocks and greenery give them a sculpturelike quality.

This town is one of the many that double their population in the summer months. When the heat rolls in, the same phenomenon takes place every year. The streets, alleys, and passages echo with the sound of footsteps, the terrace bars resume business after the recess and fill with crowds, and the shops display their wares on the sidewalks. The town is bubbling with activity and bustle. At night music from the open bars and summer parties lingers in the air. The silence of winter fades from memory.

One of these garden terraces is located at the foot of a great stone wall topped by a house. Inside, a swimming pool has been constructed. This canal-shaped swimming pool follows the wall around the edge of the garden in such a way that the water is practically in contact with the stone; it is only separated by a rim that allows you to walk between the two planes, with the heavy rock structure above you.

The rigidly right-angled swimming pool reinforces the harsh geometry of the architecture and the wall. The option of constructing a curved pool was ruled out because it would not have blended in so well with the existing architectural context.

The reflection in the water plane extends the wall, doubling its height and the vertical sensation. If we go to the water's edge and dive in, we are submerged in the vast space of rock and water.

Between the porch and the garden

Architect: Francisco Fogaz
Casa de Campo. La Romana. Dominican Republic

Often the quality of the architecture is measured by the small details. The composition and general distribution are important, as are the transition spaces between the different areas of the house. In principal these areas do not have a concrete function but, in the final analysis, they give the residence its character and resolve many design questions.

The way a house opens up to the outside tells us something not only about the architecture but also about its surroundings. A compact, opaque house with few windows or doors would be protecting itself from a hostile environment. At the opposite extreme, a dwelling that is divided into two blocks, creating in between a series of open spaces that include terraces, patios, and porches, means that we are in a temperate climate in which it is only natural that we go from indoors to outdoors every now and then.

When an architect is dreaming up the façades of a house he or she must not think of them as merely walls with windows. They are transition lines against or through which the light filters or bounces. It is too harsh on the eyes to go directly from the interior to the bright outside light.

Here the porch fulfils this function. Instead of entering the house directly, one can pause in the entrance, or vice versa. Just on the edge of the shade we can find the swimming pool, which is a second step on the way into the open air. If we are under the porch, ceramic paving stones, creepers, plants, and flowerpots all make us feel as if we are in a garden, although we are still sheltered by the architecture. The plane of water always generates a circular space, not in the strictly geometric sense but in the sense that it is a space organized around a nucleus of activity: in this case bathing and swimming. The swimming pool is also a source of luminosity: It reflects the sunlight onto the house.

Water is a medium that offers fascinating aestheic effects. As it is colorless, transparent, and mobile, it is reflected in a thousand ways. Sometimes it shimmers and at other times it is a motionless mirror, but always it is a source of beauty that does not allow you to forget it. Here the water space is surrounded by a patterned frieze that breaks the uniformity of the colors and evokes the mosaic decorations of the classic baths.

The edge of the porch is marked by round pillars that support the roof.

In this shady area, tables and wicker chairs for relaxing from the heat and sun have been set out.

The garden and the city

Designer: Pepe Cortés
Barcelona. Spain

The slow-moving, smog-belching cities seem to be designed to try our patience. They are cement and asphalt labyrinths where we live, cramped into little flats amid the agressive hustle: the "maddening crowd." The image of a beehive comes to mind. Urbanism and architecture are two disciplines that set out to make the city landscape more habitable and human. However, rarely do original ideas materialize according to their initial conception. Profit margins and other pragmatic considerations tend to get in the way. It is acceptable to use land set aside for public parks—green lungs in the gray jungle—or for playgrounds for other construction, and the high hopes disappear. The city becomes a tightly packed maze of streets, divided into parts that do not always fit together and snarl traffic.

Barcelona is a vivid example of the application of an urban plan that went astray. The ensanche area was distorted with the passage of time and the idea of making the interior squares between the blocks of houses into open spaces for recreation did not succeed. They were filled up with parking lots or even buildings. Today there is greater sensibility concerning subjects like preserving the urban landscape and efforts have been made to save part of the city for its residents. The interior of some blocks, the terraces and wide sidewalks, the alleys and the cute little squares are some of the measures taken to minimize the concrete. Simultaneously, residents try to create in their own homes, small though they may be, cozy microcosms. They aim at surrounding themselves with plants or a wall covered by creepers. We feel better if we shut out prying looks and shrill noise from our little world. We want to close off the terrace so that we can have a cup of coffee in private.

If we have enough space, we can make a garden to measure, and even go as far as putting in a little swimming pool to help us endure the hot summer in the city. The construction must be discrete and light. Around the pool there is a wood-board flooring, the type often used for designing parks and city playgrounds, marking the transition from building to garden. It has an inviting look, halfway between the hardness of the concrete and the soft grass, which has made it a favorite of architects. Treated properly, it can be well preserved and can become even more attractive with wear, which enhances its color and texture.

Terraces and other similar spaces can be
turned into gardens which oxygenate
an atmosphere contaminated by traffic
and general urban density.

The inside circle

Lleida. Spain

In some climates and at some times of the year, we find ourselves forced indoors to play or engage in sports. The temperature can dip so far that it is impossible to practice certain sports outside, swimming being a prime example. You have to have Spartan blood if you swim outdoors in winter.

Architecture can solve this problem. You can build an indoor swimming pool with a roof that keeps the harsh elements out. What is specially important is that the air-conditioning be at the right level and the water be neither too hot nor too cold. An enclosed swimming pool greatly increases the humidity, making the heat very uncomfortable.

Indoor swimming pools are areas within the house where architects can show what they are worth or, alternatively, reveal their weaknesses. They must know how to play with the few elements they have at hand. Water, light, and the surface around the pool have to be combined intelligently to produce a luminous atmosphere that does not give off a cluttered or overly introverted sensation. Too much openness must also be avoided. The architect has to reconcile beauty with comfort.

The carpentry work that runs around the swimming pool follows the circular shape, together with the grand windows, which allow us to behold the forest. The advantage of this configuration is that while we are having a bath at a cozy temperature, we can contemplate a landscape so beautiful that it makes us feel good. This is the perfect state in which to forget all about everyday cares and burdens.

When a large indoor area has to be roofed in the absence of pillars, it is necessary to design a structure that transfers the weight to the perimeter. With this pool you can appreciate the metal beam structure, like thorns, supported by the façade columns, slightly behind the carpentry work. This semicircular space stimulates people to move and encourages swimmers to travel the length of the pool to find out what is at the other end. You cannot take it all in from one point.

Glass has been chosen to finish off the space because of its transparency, which enables it to create reflections that play on the water's surface. In so doing it becomes the essence of the project. Together, in this swimming pool, glass and water create the light.

Right next to the living room

Designer: Tonet Sunyer
Barcelona. Spain

In this project, time and movement are vital parameters of modern architecture. The design is not static; it encourages physical activity.

The Mediterranean climate affords mild temperatures thanks to the influence of the sea, which softens the extremes of winter and summer. However, one of the characteristics of this climate, which can be considered a plus or a minus, is the intense and continuous solar radiation. Year-round, and especially in summer, the sun beats down for many hours. Except for sun worshippers, everybody seeks protection under trees or in some other shady spot to avoid getting burned.

The façade of this house is dominated by glass that has been re-covered with wooden slats which act as a filter. Outside, the garden can be divided in two: The part nearest the house is covered by clear-colored rock flagstones which reflect the sunlight and, therefore, do not get so hot. Around the rest of the garden grass has been planted.

If we stroll around the house we will find many different corners where we can take a break, sit down, and contemplate the architecture from diverse viewpoints. On one side there is a small swimming pool that reflects the brick wall next to it. The color range of the materials crosses a whole palette of rich hues. Every element represents a fine brushstroke that changes the texture. The rock stone is smooth and noble. The bricks are rough and harsh. The soft water ripples gently. The breeze caresses the fresh grass. Everything adds up to transmit a rich, peaceful sensation that entices us to sit down in the wooden chairs next to the table in front of the house and while away the time.

In this swimming pool the water is in contact with the house wall, which makes it clear that it is part of the overall concept. The perception that water has been used as an architectual ingredient is apparent. Inside the residence the room is lit by a powerful reflection. As the light is reflected off the water, it floods in in gentle vibrations. From the living room we watch the swimmers bathing on the other side. Separated by the crystal, we clearly see their images but their sounds are muffled by the window. The light comes in through the different filters, making the design elements stand out on the wooden pavement.

The architecture does not stop at the outside walls; instead its lines, surfaces, and structures gradually incorporate the garden into the house. These spaces take on their full glory when you walk around. If you merely stand still and look you do not get the full effect of their beauty.

The pavement around the edges of the swimming pool, where the ladders into the pool are located, is made of wooden planks, like a jetty, which give a warm touch to the house.

A privileged position

Colera. Spain

A pool not only is associated with physical activity, it also can be beautiful in its own right and often is the most fascinating aspect of the garden. Considered from this `point of view, pools fulfill the same goal as earlier decorative ponds. The calm water surface refines all of the cultivated areas around the house, and adds to the sense of relaxation. However, swimming pools must not be in the direct line of view from the accesses to the house in order to ensure the swimmers' privacy.

Modern architecture can effectively provide such privacy by isolating the entrances and bathrooms from the reception area and the main room. In this way it is easy to see that the swimming pool should be situated in a part of the garden that is sheltered from intruding views while remaining close to the porches and terraces that extend the interiors of the house outside.

The building shields the pool from the wind. Elements from the garden enrich the visual effect: Fences, trees, and architectural features like walls embellish the setting.

The wind affects the different areas in distinct ways and, therefore, they must be studied separately. Generally, the parts of the pool that are near the sea should be left open to the beach; they will enjoy the refreshing or warm breezes that blow in. However, it is necessary to guard against the dust bowl blasts, inopportunely hot or cold, that can come from inland. As the pool is most heavily used in the morning and late afternoon, the most privileged orientation is at midday. Trees have not been planted close to the swimming pool because dead leaves destroy the purity of the water.

Since the beginning of civilization, many have acknowledged the beneficial effects of bathing. It relaxes, drives out toxins, and improves the hydration of the body, producing a feeling of well-being. Bathing is one of the pleasures of everyday life, and to ensure this gratification the swimming pool must be maintained and the water kept clean.

The chemical equilibrium of the water is a key factor in controlling the dust particles that are suspended therein; they are normally visible and tend to mar or cloud the transparency. They can be eliminated by filtering. There are also microorganisms that can appear—algas, bacteria, fungi—and therefore must be treated. The water is constantly filtered and regenerated by a purifying system.

The pavement around the edges of the swimming pool is comprised of wooden planks, like a jetty, which give a warm touch to the house.

Keep in shape

Miami. Florida. USA

In this small pavilion, before having a swim, we can work out a little with weight machines, which form a line along one side near the entrance door. Once we have toned up our muscles we can dive into the pool to do some lengths.

An indoor swimming pool is expensive to build. However, it has many advantages in countries where the climate is extreme, for it can be used without interruption year-round. So that the dip or the swim is gratifying, the temperature, of both the air and the water, must vary very little from the so-called comfort temperature.

This rectangular pavilion covers two swimming pools of different sizes. A row of windows, which begin at a height of six feet, allow the afternoon sunbeams to stream through and bounce off the surface of the water, creating dancing patterns on the walls as the swimmers do their lengths. The façade opposite the entrance door is completely transparent, offering an outside view with all its green and blue tones. You cannot help glancing out through these windows. On the other walls the sensation of movement is maintained by a changing design of different colored ceramic tiles, as if the wall were splattered with little vibrating spots of color which become more diffuse as they rise.

When choosing the material for the bottom of the swimming pool it is necessary to select carefully, bearing in mind the effect that has to be achieved. Here the same treatment as that used on the walls has been chosen, with the addition of a geometric pattern reminiscent of the mosaics of the ancient Roman baths.

As central pillars would not fit into this space, the roof is built with large metal beams running into the side walls.

When we engage in outdoor sports, the fresh air, clear sky, and luminosity of the sunshine are a plus. If a cold day obliges us to take exercise indoors, it is better to do so with strong daylight, a view of the panorama, and good ventilation.

An intimate garden

Designer: Galper-Baldon
Los Angeles. California. USA

This space has been designed to please all five senses. The playful, vibrant reflections of the colors and the swaying of the leaves attract our eyes.

On Sunset Boulevard, in Los Angeles, California, camouflaged by lush vegetation, we can find this residence, which was designed to imitate the style of the Spanish villas. Twenty years after its construction, the owners decided to build a swimming pool. As very little land was available the pool was placed close to the house, on a plot that is approximately seventy-five by eighteen feet surrounded by a small patio garden where bamboo abounds. The swimming pool juts out of the pavement, at which point there is a surrounding wall covered in stone. This low wall, used as a bench and as a ledge, separates the water surface from the rest of the elements, while allowing you to go as near as possible to the water without falling in. On top of this wall are some porticos that go from one side of the swimming pool to the other and can support creepers if necessary.

The thick vegetation means that the sunshine is filtered into rich nuances of color when it reaches the surface of the water, an effect reminiscent of a garden vegetable plot. The tradition of cultivating fruit trees, laurels, cypresses, or pergolas with vines that began in the Middle Ages continues. In the Gothic period, fruit trees were associated with holy places, like the cloisters of the convents and cathedrals, or with gardens of official buildings or palaces.

Here the aim was to reproduce the atmosphere of silence and meditation that has always been linked to these patios. Time passes slowly. Light filters through the leaves, highlighting their colors. The vegetation isolates us from the city and creates a relaxing microclimate. The temperature is milder and a pacific breeze picks up, inviting us to spend more time outdoors.

In one of the corners of the garden there is a small pond where ferns and other water plants grow. Here the water is darker, a somewhat green tone with white dots of stone and rock that brings to mind the Japanese gardens where water and rocks are laid out symbolically.

The contrast between the silence
and the noise of the fountain, the
scents of the different flowers
planted around the swimming pool
and the texture of the rocks, the
wood, or the water, all help us to
feel that we are in a special place.
Everything enriches our sensations
when we are in contact with nature.

The domestic oasis

Mark Adams Residence
Palm Springs. California. USA

The garden comes into view like an oasis in the desert. The aridity of the mountains, the blinding light, and the extremely hot or cold air are transformed when the water appears. When a stretch of desert is watered or has underground water sources it becomes a small, clearly defined paradise. When shade comes into play the heat is mitigated, the air becomes more humid, and the place is less hostile. This small, artificially set-up oasis around a swimming pool is an example of how humans can modify the environment beneficially.

A series of constructions hide the swimming pool from prying eyes. On the other side the perspective is wide open, taking in all the surrounding mountains. A part of the garden has been cobbled with rustic ceramic tiles. This pavement adds a touch of color and enriches the texture, especially as the smoothness of the water contrasts with the rough ceramic.

The porches extend the dwelling out to the bathing area. They are vital in this hot environment, for they offer shade and prevent the air from becoming stifling, reducing the sensation of suffocating heat.

When we want to enter the pool a slightly submerged platform allows us to go in bit by bit as we descend the stairs. On one side a little wall has been built separating part of the swimming pool to form a children's pool. On top of the mountain slope, which dies away a few yards from the pavement, chaise lounges, tables, and umbrellas are laid out, enabling you to rest and tranquilly idle away your leisure time. The frontier between the bathing area and the mountain is marked by a stone wall that encircles the perimeter of the oasis. The palm trees surge out of a somewhat chaotic vegetation mass. Their thin trunks open up like white umbrellas into treetops that provide welcome shade over the aperitif tables and the benches where you can relax.

The textures and colors of the
vegetation that is watered
regularly are more varied.
To create a garden with
personality one has to know
how to combine both elements.

The vegetation planted around the swimming pool contrasts with the indigenous greenery. Wide-open spaces without water are characterized by hard-leaved plants, often prickly or thorned, to keep animals away from the water they have inside. These plants are like sculptures.

Very close to the water's edge there is a row of plants that divides the bathing area from the path. If we should perchance look up before diving into the water, the panorama is fantastic. It seems as if we are in a real oasis, miles away from any type of civilization.

Although the landscape is rugged and sparsely populated, the architecture uses a familiar language. The building is traditional in its organization, structure, and materials and seeks to create a microclimate of safety and comfort—a space that humankind controls, dedicated to pleasure and leisure.

This indoor pool, just like the classic baths, is presided over by a grand mirror that reflects the light from the water.

An Asian touch

Designer: Leach + Leach
San Francisco. California. USA

As if we were in a labyrinth of mirrors we come to the central space. The dancing reflections from the water and the glass fill the air with flashes of light. The light enters through the crystal doors and shines on the mosaic that presides over the swimming pool. All the paths flow like little streams of water that finally reach the lake.

In Asian culture, bathing had a religious significance: It was an act of purification before praying. The water, the fountains, and the spas all formed part of the architecture, just as the salons, dining rooms, bedrooms, and patios did. There were even buildings dedicated exclusively to bathing, called *hamam* in Arabic.

The spaces where the swimming pools were situated had to have natural light, which came in through skylights in the roof. This protected the swimmers from people looking in but did not deprive them of light. The materials used were humidity proof. Marble, ceramics, and granites were combined harmoniously in a straightforward and tasteful composition.

This indoor pool has succeeded in maintaining the spirit inherited from the classical period. The columns have elegant capitals, bases, abacusses, and arcades. Although these elements no longer have their original structural function, they are used for decoration. Doing things like this can always provoke debate in architecture. However, a pleasant ambience is created thanks to the spaciousness and the lighting.

The outside landscape has been brought inside a little with some plants to add variety of color to the numerous materials already present.

The rim has been marked out with dark ceramic, which contrasts with the mosaic of the pavement around the pool and inside it.

The sensation of amplitude one receives on entering this space is reinforced by the clear tones used to cover the ceiling. The stillness is total until someone dives into the water and then a noise that reminds us of breaking glass reverberates. In an instant the geometric mosaic pattern disappears beneath the ripples and waves only return a few moments later.

The interior decoration combines several materials, all of which stand up to the humidity.

From the pool

Designer: Wallace Neff
Beverly Hills. California. USA

This great mansion in the country harks back to the techniques and the aesthetics of traditional architecture. The roof is tiled, the porches have arcades, the windows are functional, and there are large eaves that offer shade from the sun. A gentle staircase leads down to the swimming pool a few yards from the house. Having the pool so near is very comfortable. It ends up forming part of everyday life and is a focus of activity, fun, and at the same time rest.

It is curious to see how the activity that goes on around the pool changes during the day. At dawn, the first rays are reflected in the calm water. The blue is transparent: It is a plane of light that surprises us when we get up and go outside before having breakfast. All around there is total calm. At midday the activity begins to liven up. As people dive in the splashes break the silence and the air fills with shouts and laughter. When the sun sets, the heat begins to relent. The water takes on an orange tone and the bottom disappears. It is time to sit down and have a drink as the day draws to a close. When the landscape is dark and the first lights come on in the living quarters, the swimming pool becomes a spectacle. The night lighting system guarantees the user's safety while converting the pool into a new and original, almost unknown, place for us.

We will be able to enjoy the mornings in the shade of the trees, the afternoons by the rivers, the sun setting in the early evening, and the starry night. When life becomes less hectic, new surprising facets of a person appear.

Some images are immediately associated with a house in the country. Living in the country means being close to nature and wanting to slow down the pace of our lives. In the modern world cities occupy center stage; the downtown pace and urban sprawl circumscribe our activities. Going to the country means freedom to engage in other types of recreation. Those who decide to construct a house on grassland, or in a meadow, or next to a wood have made a decision. They want to isolate themselves, lead a more tranquil life, and start a double journey: going back to simple basics and leaving behind all the ties and obligations that city life imposes.

The countryside is more than just an idyllic
scene. The houses have a recognizably
precise but functional form, blending
into the landscape and defining the relationship between the habitants and their houses.

The environment is very alluring. The greenery grows over the architecture, softening the angles and diluting the boundary between nature and construction.

Between two butresses

Designer: Àngels Garcia Giró
Peratallada. Spain

The swimming pools of today are the final result of a tradition that began with the ancient baths. These were installed in gardens and houses of the nobility in Egypt, Persia, India, and Rome. They were an essential part of Arab architecture. In some regions the tradition of combining rock with water has been maintained for cultural and climatic reasons. The water plane is incorporated into the architecture like one more element of the composition.

This carefully designed swimming pool is situated between the two butresses of a country house in the county of Empordà, near the city of Girona. The location has not been random. The architect deliberately chose to place side by side these two materials, rock and water, to contrast their textures, their color, and the very different ways in which they reflect light.

Swimming pools are landscape elements that help to organize the garden space. However, they must be in harmony with the construction and the so-called soft architecture in order to blend into the environment. The "soft architecture" is composed of pavements, steps, platforms, and pergolas to filter the light.

With the pool protected and bordered by the butresses, a beautiful and interesting plastic effect is achieved. The reflection in the water multiplies, making the architecture more sublime. The stone becomes lighter, and the water is restless, giving off little sparkles.

When we go into the water we sense the difference between the two materials. The walls are made of rock, which is unbreachable, but the water opens up to receive us. We enter the world created by the architecture.

The project sets out to take advantage of the contrast between the language of traditional buildings and that of modern architecture, bringing the two worlds together until they are joined physically.

The water plane is framed by the solidity of the wall and the butresses. The textures of the stone and water contrast with and complement each other.

A platform of wooden boards
reinforces the horizontality of the
swimming pool, creating a perfect
ambience in which to unwind and
soak up the sun and nature.

The patterns created by the
reflections enrich the
architecture. If we are on the
raised platform we have a
fantastic view over the fields
and the entrance path.

Around the house there are crop fields that are like immense carpets that change color with the seasons.

As in all country houses, horticulture is crucial. An effort has been made to introduce elements that do not need too much attention and that add a rough, rugged touch to the landscape.

Near and comfortable

Tuscany. Italy

The steps that lead us gently down into the water seem to be a natural extension of the garden.

This small swimming pool in the garden of a detached family house livens up the outside area with the bright light of its water. The wall covering consists of small ceramic tiles in different tones of blue. This type of ceramic tile is called earthenware and produces a vibrating luminous effect, as if the water were always gently sending ripples across the surface. Little flickers of light dance on the surface.

As the pool is in an L shape, two areas are created. One is the access, where some steps lead us gently down into the water, and the other is the bathing area. This staggered effect is similar to what we could find in the two levels of a garden. The steps, which are in one corner of the pool, allow us to enter the water gradually. The edges of the steps are marked with white tiles so that they are easier to see.

In spite of being rectangular, the angles have been softened by slightly curving the sides. It looks as if the pressure of the water has pushed back the swimming pool walls. Wooden flooring that runs up to the beginning of the grass at one end and to the ceramic tiles on another side has been laid down around the edge of the pool.

The scale of the elements in this garden is in proportion with the residences. The furniture, the distances, and the sizes are a prolongation of the measurements inside the house. The dimension of the landscape, the forest, and the horizon remain on the other side beyond the wall. The world in which the summer life of the family occurs is peaceful: Nothing can disturb the calm, and light is everywhere.The shadows have been pushed aside; nothing is unknown.

When we look at this garden, children at play come to mind. It is a space designed for families, for a harmonious and wholesome life where everything is out in the open and there are no dark corners.

What summer means

Sheltered by the pergola, we can settle down to enjoy breakfast while looking out at the garden.

If we were asked what our image of happiness was, the scene that would come to mind is not far from what is evoked in these photos. There would be a large country house with little outbuildings surrounding an immaculately tended garden, freshly cut grass, a picturesque path, flower beds awash with colorful petals, indigenous trees overhead, the bent trunk of an olive tree or cypresses standing upright, and most important of all, the vacations stretching out ahead of us.

The climbing plants are starting to invade the pergola: They go up the pillars and gently wrap themselves around the wood, offering us the shade that helps us to make it through the summer. In spring, these creepers burst into flower and carpet the walls with pretty colors. The trees rise above the house and the geometry of their branches, more fragile and mobile the higher up they are, converts the sky into an infinite number of brilliant blue fragments.

We can choose between having breakfast on the porch or under the pergola. On the porch there is a lot of shade to protect us from the excessive heat of the summer. If we sit under the pergola the light reaches us after filtering through the creepers. There is no better way to start the day. Being able to carry out daily activities in the open air is a privilege we can enjoy thanks to the mild climate of the region. Tables and wicker chairs help to create different atmospheres. The architectual landscape is characterized by its variety, and we can change the mood by changing places.

The flooring that goes around the swimming pool is composed of a pattern of ceramic pieces that plays with two colors and two sizes. The lowness of the house and the spaciousness of the garden work together to make it a pleasant place to be.

In this house the relationship with nature comes into play in a way that is distinct from the majority of residences. Here, it is not nature that surrounds the house, but

In this experimental garden different examples of the vegetation that grow naturally in this climate have been planted. However, they will not require a great deal of special care for the weather is mild. The garden is magnificent and practical: It does not try to offer an exhibition nor an exotic display.

rather the house that encircles nature. The grass and the trees are center stage, in the middle of the house, while the architecture is at the edge, cutting off an offshoot of an old forest. From the swimming pool onward the ceramic pavement gives way to grass where we can lie right down on the ground to enjoy the pleasant scent of the greenery.

White atop green

Italy

There is a style of architecture that tries not to intrude on the landscape. Its materials belong to the earth, its forms blend into the contours of the land, and its colors make up a harmonic palette. However, there is also another way of doing things which can produce very different and interesting results.

In some projects the aim is to put into practice a hard-hitting idea that stands out because of the contrast. It could even set out to change the landscape around it. This is the case at hand.

This residence is not a compact entity; rather it is spread out over the land, incorporating the empty spaces into its layout. The border between inside and outside disappears. There is no line drawn; instead there are areas where we can walk freely.

The house, on its thin platform, appears to be fighting against the mountain. The pavement marks the beginning of the private territory. The whiteness stands out against the landscape. It gives us security and from here we can look out over the coastline and the sea in the background. The living areas are around the perimeter. Intermittently, modern pergolas, balconies, porticos, and porches liven up the house. Within this shiny white compound there are two pools where we can have a dip and cool off. The two planes of water are reflections that complement the architecture: They are two blue dashes to rest our eyes on. They look as if they have been designed by someone from ancient Greece, for they are surrounded by clasically proportioned statues. Or perhaps they seem like part of a photography set that was built for shooting an advertisement emulating a world of elegance and good looks.

From outside we can see how the architecture has caught a tree in its spider web. The forms of the branches become thinner and more twisted as we ascend the slope. The dark color of the bark contrasts with the clarity of the pillars and the beams that appear to frame the image, as if it were a painting. Inside this artificial territory of lines that are so clean and of abstract forms, we have the sensation that we are observers of nature looking down from a higher point. We see nature in harmony. The brusque, violent, unleashed part does not reach us for it has been filtered out so that it is more human, rational, and ordered. This is one option among the many that architecture can take.

This artificial composition of clean, abstract lines makes it seem as though we are observing nature from a higher point.

Within this white compound are two dazzling pools where we can cool off with a dip.

Extending the living room

Deulder. France

The table prepared for breakfast is only separated by sliding glass panes.

When in the same space different elements that are associated with the open air are mixed with other fixtures that we always find inside, a strange atmosphere is created. A wall lined with paintings belongs naturally in the living room of a house, next to armchairs and a dining table in a cozy atmosphere. In contrast, swimming pools imply physical activity: They are associated with movement, exertion, the noise of splashing water, and the open air.

Combining both atmospheres, this project is disorienting and initially disconcerting. For an instant we do not know if we are in a living room or have gone out into the garden. The architectural limits have become flexible; the decoration is no longer orthodox. As the rules have been changed, water appears where we were not expecting it. Not one sign tells us what the function of this space is—only the presence of water. The materials and the objects that surround it are no different from those that could be formed around a table.

Once we have caught on that the project is winking at us, we will be able to take in some original details. The sunlight pours in through some great crystal panes that show us the garden. The structure that has to bear the weight of the forged decoration is slightly off the façade. The round pillars take the weight and the seals are unobtrusive. The crystal goes right down from the ceiling to the floor. At one end it can be opened and you can pass into the garden. At night a row of lights provides the illumination. Their reflection divides the pool into two, as if there were two lanes, a two-way street for swimming.

We can imagine how comfortable it would be to have our own pool as we come out of the living room, just crossing the passage. We would not even need to take cover were it raining. The temperature is ideal to start everyday, before work, with a few lengths of breaststroke or crawl. The whole body would be gently toned up before the daily grind. In the middle of the wall with the paintings there is a window that enables us to watch what is going on. The reflecting light patterns from the water come in through the window, playing on the ceiling and wall.

The separating line between inside
and outside has become flexible.

Corners bathed in
sunlight and shady areas
create a varied garden.

The outbuildings surround a central area in which the swimming pool is located.

Around the water's edge

Axel Verwoot. Belgium

This reconverted country residence is divided into different buildings that were previously used for agricultural labor. In the central patio, where the threshing floor was normally found, there is a pool surrounded by porches and areas totally exposed to the sun. Protected from the forest by the outline of the house, the water is not contaminated by the leaves and receives enough sunlight to make it appear as a blue plane between the stone and the trees.

A country house turned into a second residence gives certain aspects priority. The pool becomes the lead player because the house is going to be principally for summer use. In the Mediterranean this season is very hot. If we are far from the beach, a pool will be an ideal way to cool off.

It used to be that the building of country houses was closely related to the rural economy. They were a solution to the problem of having to live near the workplace. In the old days this was even more important as the means of transportation were slow. This reality also explains why small outbuildings are dotted around near the crops far away from the main house and the nearby villages. Farmhouses, when they were built, were designed for various perfectly defined functions, both indoors and outdoors: The corrals, the henhouses, the wine cellars, and the tool shed all formed a part of the dwelling. Thus the whole farm was a business unit, which included the surrounding forests, fields, pastures, outbuildings, and even the irrigation ditches and nearby millponds. Therefore, the farm was a firm with a double purpose: cover the basic necessities of the family and participate in the market economy as a supplier.

Farms are often characterized by the space between the different buildings. Here, three factors have played a role: the search for water, the need to be near the woods, and the topography.

Today city and town dwellers have converted these rural constructions into leisure homes. They are second residences in which to relax, disconnect from work and stress, and dedicate time to the family, friends, and peace. However, sometimes these retreats are used for subsidary activities.

It is this attitude that enables people to enjoy their freedom and to have a vacation that is faithful to the etymological root of the word: In Latin "vacare" means "to be empty, vacant."

Harmony and health

Sydney. Australia

Around the swimming pool there are some reclining deck chairs where we can rest. From them we can take in the beauty and harmony of the functional interior architecture and the city skyline.

In today's society the cult of body worship has taken off. Right from childhood we are bombarded with messages about how we should look. The media are the champions of this crusade against looking out of shape, or having wrinkles. The goal is to control nature and hold back the years, halting the effect that the passage of time has on us. This is the message.

The best way is to play a sport often and hard. And to visit the so-called health and beauty centers where there are infinite treatments. These fitness centers have very complete installations and their look and image are not left to chance. The little details are carefully thought out; the materials are top quality, smooth, and noble. The colors have to fit in with the activity or the sport in which we are engaging, and to help us relax our mind meanwhile.

Besides having different rooms in which weights, aerobics, or fitness can be practiced, there are also areas set aside for swimming, Turkish baths, or saunas. Some fortunate people are able to constuct these installations in their own homes.

The visual effect as we walk into the room is enchanting. The room has been organized around the pool in a symmetrical composition: An intense sensation of equilibrium is transmitted. It is divided into three spaces as if they were naves of a temple. The largest space, which accommodates the water plane, is covered over by a vault roof in which embedded spotlights have been placed like stars in the firmament.

The columns divide up and organize the three sections. This artificial firmament is reflected in the pool. The swimmer can be floating in the water like a night bird, or swimming in the sea beneath the starlit sky.

The vaulted roof makes us feel as if we were outside. In this way the roof has been made to disappear, just as in the baroque churches in which they painted the ceilings, camouflaged the architecture, and multiplied the sensation of height.

The reflection of the architecture

Architect: Norman Cinnamond
Sant Cugat. Spain

The setting of the house and garden employs a whole palette of colors, from the range of greens, reddish tones, and blues right through to the white lines that structure the composition.

Situated in a forested Mediterranean landscape near the coast, the house rises up in the middle of a clearing. The color of the façades, the windows framed in white, and the purity of the lines contrast with the humid and dark image of the forest. Before the house there lays a magnificent swimming pool as wide as the living room of the lodge.

The relationship between the living area and the swimming pool is evident. The large windows can be opened, leaving the fine curtains to flutter like sails in the wind. We can almost hear the chords of the music that stray through the night air from the summer party. The forest is silent and the moon transparently clear while the illuminated house casts shadows outside.

The initial project was to rehabilitate and extend an isolated family dwelling constructed around the beginning of the century. The house showed signs of neglect. While the original design and structure were respected, new formal elements that resolved both the aesthetic and distribution problems were incorporated.

The size of the dwelling makes an impact: It appears as a compact entity that is perforated in some places and includes a transparent stairwell. The interior layout has given the house a new image while creating a new relationship between the four floors. The space, open and fluid, goes up to the attic and allows daylight to enter everywhere.

The nineteenth-century style of the house has been conserved and the new elements that have been introduced harmonize with the old. Classicism also makes itself felt in the way that the swimming pool has been approached. The house extends into the garden in the form of a pavement of flagstones, like a carpet laid down on the grass. The swimming pool contrasts with the texture of the stone, and the reflection in its waters throws back the image of its columns and balustrade.

Around the swimming pool a pavement of wood, reminiscent of jetties, has been placed. Beneath our feet the wood creaks as it gently gives: The contact is pleasant as we walk barefoot to the edge to dive into the water. If it is good-quality wood, and well looked after, these boards give great results.

A double curve

Rimini. Italy

This swimming pool is inspired by the natural layout of the land, the lakes, the ponds, and the still waters of the rivers. However, when it is contemplated as a finished piece, so neat and orderly, one can see that an effort has been made to differentiate it from the landscape.

This is a fine example of a swimming pool that takes advantage of different types of curves. The layout changes as we go around the edge: There is a display of convex and concave lines that bring the landscape to life. This clearing among the thick vegetation is an ordered space with few elements. Sometimes a more enchanting atmosphere is created by introducing just a few resources rather than by cluttering up a space. The simplicity allows each part of the whole to enjoy its own light.

These different curves mark off areas inside the swimming pool. At one end the circle closes and a shallow swimming pool is set aside for the young chidren. This swimming pool belongs to a campsite situated in a shady corner of a forest. As the installations are used continuously, it was necessary to employ resistant, easy-to-maintain, and hygienic materials. The area around the swimming pool is paved because grass is too fragile and would soon be scuffed up.

The campers can rest in front of the swimming pool beneath straw umbrellas. While the parents have something to drink they can supervise the children's games, always close enough to avoid any accidents that may happen. This is when the social activity around the swimming pool is at its height.

These swimming pools were constructed like curved containers by using the technique of gunned concrete (also called shotcrete). It is a rapid and useful system, for there are no expansion joints, meaning that the seal is tighter.

Realizing projects with this type of concrete is an art that requires a great deal of practical experience. The concrete is produced with a premanufactured mix. It is then placed in a "shooting machine" which guns out the concrete through a directed nozzle, or jet, by means of air impulsion. The concrete hits the surface to which it is being applied with such force that it sticks and becomes more compact. The rim of the swimming pool is a decorative frame that defines the pool's form more sharply. A dark-colored, vitrified ceramic pattern marks the curve as if it were a felt-tip highlighter on paper.

MEDITERRANEAN SWIMMING POOLS

These pools are on the Mediterranean coast. The presence of the sea in the background, slopes covered with holm oaks and pines, low shrub vegetation, and sweet-smelling grasses make up a typical landscape which enjoys a sunny, fairly dry climate. In the majority of these cases the pool is located near the slope or precipice so that the maximum visual effect is achieved. The mountainside is then staggered into terraces with rock borders, steps, and gardened slopes. This is how the outside part of the houses has been organized. In this climate the light is very intense and the air is clean and bright. The sharp colors form fine contrasts. These are all good reasons why it is difficult to stay indoors, where it is always darker, and thus most activity takes place in the open air.

This chapter will take us to the northeast Spanish coast in Girona, the Greek Spetsai coast, the French Riviera, and the Balearic Islands.

Like a boat

Architect: Norman Cinnamond
Sa Riera. Girona. Spain

The tops of the pine trees stick out, framing the Mediterranean behind them.

There are residences that are special not just because of the large land plot they occupy or their layout, or because of the quality of their materials, but simply because of their location and the way they fit into the landscape.

On the steep slope of a typical Mediterranean mountainside, covered in rocks and pines, with the shimmering sea as the backdrop, this house is a fine vantage point over the waves. It can be compared to a boat anchored in the middle of the Mediterranean, looking out over the horizon. The topography favors the organization of the architecture into superimposed, staggered terraces that reach down to a few yards from the shoreline.

The swimming pool is located on one of these terraces, as an extension of the first floor. Its personality is related to the architecture of the house: The same design criteria have been used and the materials match the overall effect.

The house blends into the landscape with the architectural aid of porches, pergolas, walls, and the swimming pool. In this way the house juts out less; it merges into the environment as its volume is softened. The porches are transition spaces, for as we walk along them, or under the galleries, it is not clear if we are in the house or not. We can feel the breeze but the architecture is sheltering us. The rain would not bother us.

The swimming pool does not break the continuity of the terrace, where the family and guests can relax and feast their eyes on the panorama. The pool is surrounded by teak boards, treated to protect them from the elements, and a white metal tube railing that is reminiscent of that on a boat. Just a little bit above our eyeline appear the crowns of the pines that shade the scene in the late afternoon and early evening.

This pool has not been dug into the garden; rather it is mounted on a forged metal support. Such a construction method is more costly, like the pools installed on building roofs. The concrete container must be perfectly sealed.

Between the shady pergola and the water there is a rectangle of grass to lie down on and soak up the sun, or simply to breathe in the aroma of grass that lingers in the air as we stroll barefoot.

The large railed terrace with a wood flooring reminds us of the deck of a boat.

The double line on the horizon

Lloret. Spain

The round shape of one end contrasts with the right angle that points at the horizon like the prow of a ship. The geometry is forceful, its symmetry being the most striking aspect.

A swimming pool can be just a simple container for water that cools us down when the heat is on. However, it is also an aesthetic element that forms part of the ambience of the residence, blending in with the greenery and the terrain, or adopting the most diverse forms and colors, and using novel materials.

On another level the swimming pool may be part of a project that seeks to solve problems with construction innovations, in which the materials complement each other and bring architectual quality to the overall concept. This pool performs both functions.

This house is surrounded by a Mediterranean forest that has been converted into a splendid garden that entices the visitor to stroll around. On the different levels there are cozy, shady, hidden areas, as well as completely exposed spots that offer an unhindered view as far as the horizon.

Here, taking advantage of the gentle slope down to the sea, a bilevel swimming pool has been constructed to produce a very precise aesthetic effect. Before our eyes two superimposed surfaces of very different colors appear: the dark background of the sea and the luminous, clear swimming pool. There is no line that separates them. They are two perfect, abstract planes. This aesthetic and refined effect is achieved thanks to the construction details. The rim has been made to disappear by gently sloping it until it is covered by the water. To collect the water that overflows, another swimming pool has been built on a lower level. This edge of the swimming pool is suspended like a balcony or a projection. The structure requires that the concrete framework be reinforced even though the load supported is not excessive. The continuous fall of the water is a third element, a little fountain that introduces a dynamic element into the garden. The constant flow sounds like leaves rustled by the wind, a gentle murmuring over the sound of the ripples and splashes.

At one end of the swimming pool some stairs lead us to another garden terrace marvelously situated to look over the sea. The greenery is planted in sloping flower beds bordered by cypresses and pines. The path zigzags down to the pool through the garden.

Going to the edge

Spetsai. Greece

The sensation that we have as we near the pavement edge is that of walking on a ship's deck. There is a sharp drop-off to where the waves are beating below, throwing up splashes of foam that come and go rhythmically.

Everything can change overnight. The light can be gray, the water greenish and opaque, or silvery and brilliant, like a darting fish.

In a summer house the design of the interior is as important as the space that surrounds it for many hours are spent outside. On this hillside by the sea the rocky landscape is covered with pines. A platform that extends as far as the edge of the slope has been constructed. No wall has been erected, so that the sensation of a vantage point and terrace is more intense. Only a pergola closes the view of the landscape. The round pillars and wooden beams provide enough shade when we look out over the terrain so that we are not blinded.

The pine trunks seem to grow out of the pavement, like the pergola columns. The reflections, shadows, and lights all play together, extending the architectural lines and merging them with the landscape. The reflections are never completely finished: They disappear when the water ripples. All the composition work is designed to transmit a single image, and to project it to the occupants. Architecture plus imagination equals fantasy. An illusion can be created by the perspective, the pavement, the terrace, and the precipice.

Both the swimming pool and the terrace have sharp angles that seem to want to anchor the architecture to the ground. If you peer over the treetops the view of the mountain from both the pool and the terrace is fantastic. The materials employed and the methods used reveal the care that has been taken. The materials introduced do not blemish nature; they try to empathize with what was already there and to rediscover connections.

The architecture has incorporated the values of a period when the relationship between humankind and the environment was one of collaboration and not domination. Nowadays, it sometimes seems that direct contact with the elements, the physical phenomena, and the quality of materials have been forgotten. Normally, an architectural project has confines, separating one property from another. Here the unique architectural element that is visible on the horizon is the pergola, which does not confine but rather subtly frames the panorama.

The architecture forms terraces on the pine-spotted hillside from where we can enjoy the singular views.

Between the sea and the sky

Costa Brava. Spain

The northern part of the Catalonian coast is an abrupt, rocky, and enormously beautiful landscape. The rocks are jagged. Occasionally there are stretches where it relents to form small inlets or coves with pebbles, which are known as "calas." The mountains go down do to the sea, while the pines have been slightly bent by the wind. The twisted trunks give away their age. The leaves and branches form a compact mass of green that at times is difficult to penetrate. The intense luminosity gives the sea a dark blue tone that spews white dots of foam as it crashes into the rocks.

This landscape is a spectacle repeated every day. If a swimming pool and house are to be built on this strip of ground between the mountain and the sea, it is almost obligatory to situate it at the edge of the precipice. The pool appears as if it wants to lean over the brink, produce strong emotions, and embellish the panorama.

Such was the goal here. Go to the limit and you will get the most out of the space. The swimming pool shape reveals this intention. The rectangle suddenly opens into a generous semicircle that reaches the cliff. It is as if the water has broken its container and caresses the ground until it touches the air. At one end, where the scent of the sea wafts over the pool, the rim is hidden to emphasize this effect. The overflowing water has to be collected below. Statues with an Asian look rim the pool, giving it a classic feeling, which is reinforced by the symmetrical disposition of the elements.

A cypress tree barrier protects the swimmers from nosy neighbors. This practical addition borrows from a local building tradition. To cut off the wind a row of these trees is planted in a strategic position nearby. They fulfill a double function: to protect against the gales and to establish the borders of the property.

As the pool is quite near the brink, when we swim we have a strange floating sensation. We are floating in the pool, while behind us the backdrop leaves us, surprisingly, suspended in the air.

Looking up from the sea we see how the walls mark off the gardened terraces with Mediterranean pines.

When night falls

Canyellas. Spain

A swimming pool is a landscape that we imagine in daylight, the water brightly reflecting the sky, the shadows of the trees, and people sunbathing until they dive in to cool off. But a swimming pool can also come into its own at night with the right lighting strategically placed both in the garden and in the water. A new scene can be brought to life. The water no longer merely reflects the light; it contains it and is converted into a beacon that lights up the surroundings.

The illumination of a pool has to offer technical security: The electricity must never come into contact with the water for safety reasons. The instructions for building a swimming pool have to be followed carefully.

When choosing the type of container that is going to hold the water we have to bear in mind the quality, form, and dimensions of the terrain. Rocky land, which is harder to clear, has the advantage of being firm enough so that the concrete foundation can be eliminated. On the other hand, there could be natural leaks, which would have to be corrected immediately. Soft and sandy soil is easy to excavate but the pool must be solidly reinforced.

The slightly curved shape of the swimming pool makes it fit into the space between the balustrade, the wall that encloses the plot, and the porch. The balustrade and the wall are whitewashed. The latter has narrow ledges which are used as flowerpots. In these openings plants grow, giving the image of a great rock out of which greenery sprouts spontaneously, geometrically disordered, haphazardly like green relief brushstrokes. Nights are part of vacation memories. Nights when the heat eases off and the terraces are full of people partying at an outdoor supper, under the moonlight. Summer parties often take place around a private swimming pool. The music and entertainment of a dance has a unique sound, as Scott Fitzgerald described in *The Great Gatsby*.

The architecture of these houses, with their pools on the rocky mountain crest, defines the coast's image. Humans have sculpted the slope, forming it to enable them to carry out their activities. Nature and artificial elements are intertwined, giving birth to a new landscape that is sometimes harmonious and sometimes discordant.

Landscape design is a recent discipline. It calls for instruments, ideas, and models that are different from those used in architecture. It works on a much larger scale and its starting point was for many years the naturalist aesthetic defined by Olmsted. It was from the seventies onward that landscape architects incorporated ecological ideas and cultural influences into their work.

Beautiful and easy to use

Architect: Norman Cinnamond
Girona. Spain

On one of the terraces above the pool, a table has been placed on top of wooden boards so that the family can fully enjoy the outdoor life.

Gardens have long existed, but the word itself, which comes from French, did not enter the Spanish language until the fifteenth century. In French it means "closed off." Logically, it refers to the "hortus conclusus," the separated garden referred to in the Bible. Perhaps the Jewish gardens were fenced off because many were in towns and the barrier protected the owners from the intrusions of other people. There were also other types of gardens: the vegetable garden or plot. Before the fifteenth century these were already in use: Flowers and plants were being cultivated exclusively for aesthetic ends, while other trees bore fruit to be eaten. The orchards also gave off a fine scent.

In the twentieth century, the naturalist ideas of romanticism spurred the creation of the first natural park in the Balearic Islands. Even today, the small private gardens of the turn of the century persist among the landscape designers with historicist ideas; sometimes the deficiencies are overcome with modernist interventions. The 1940s were marked by the return to fashion of the Italian style, which had left its mark on gardens over the centuries through the Renaissance, mannerism, baroque, and neoclassic styles.

This swimming pool and garden reveal the influence of the island traditions—the Balears were "visited" by many traders and armies—in the blending of styles in a careful and practical composition. The rural buildings put the emphasis on functionality, and this has been extended to the new elements.

The swimming pool has been fitted into the softly sloping landscape by adapting the topography with walls and gardened terraces. Often releveling the ground is more expensive than building the swimming pool itself. However, it is always necessary. Around the pool the water is separated from the grass by a ceramic rock pavement, a very common element in these country houses. At one end of the swimming pool the edge appears to be a few inches below the water plane. This is a costly but beautiful visual effect: It appears as if the water were a solid and did not need to be held back.

If you go from the house to the pool you pass by a sculpturelike hedge of bushes. The entrance to the bathing area is under an arch of creepers. Every now and then cypresses stand out straight and tall. These thick vertical lines are reference points for the observer, enabling him or her to measure the distances.

The well-cared-for garden makes the composition lines very clean. They are well defined, like pure geometric figures.

A style exercise

Marrakech. Morocco

Swimming in your own private pool is a luxury reserved for only a few privileged people.

The materials used and the geometry of the interior dimensions have to allow for the resonance and the amplification of sounds that a plane of water will produce.

Because of the abundant condensation produced by the high humidity level, the air has to be treated.

The forerunner of the pool was the baths. In ancient Egypt, Persia, or Byzantium, baths and spas were a central part of the predominant culture and of the architecture. The Greeks and the Romans continued the custom, leaving their heritage to the Europeans and Americans.

During the classical period people had a direct relationship with water. All the ancient civilizations were established around the Mediterranean and many of them were fertilized by rivers, like the Euphrates, the Tigris, and the Nile. In Ancient Greece swimming and bathing were common habits reflected in mythology and in history. The rapport with the sea was part of the Hellenic cult of physical beauty and thus bathing came to be one of the customs that characterized life, both in the rivers, on the plentiful Greek beaches, and in the ornamental ponds, the true forerunner of the swimming pools. In Ancient Rome the thermal baths were the most favored of official meeting places.

Architecturally, designing an indoor swimming pool is an exercise in style that entails overcoming technical difficulties because the acoustic and visual effects are awkward to control.

To execute a successful project it is necessary to think simultaneously about the interior architectual elements and the plane of the water that is going to be contained. The volumes, the composition, the materials, and the coverings will have to be compatible with the initial concept.

In Nordic climates the indoor pool is a necessity. In winter people seek warmth, intimacy, and a place to hide from the outdoor elements. In summer, they try to introduce outside elements indoors. The choice of materials has to take this duality into consideration. The coverings of the area around the pool soften the hardness of the construction materials. The surfaces are leveled off and given a more decorative look. In this indoor swimming pool the antihumidity resistence of the walls and the ceiling has been a major concern. The ventilation system plays a decisive role in maintaining a comfortable temperature.

A waterfall

Lloret de Mar. Spain

Besides enhancing the decoration, this six-foot cascade-fountain is also relaxing to behold.

Enjoying their own swimming pool is an aspiration that many downtown residents have. This desire starts with the wish to own a hideaway in the country or near the beach where they can go from time to time to get things off their mind. They like the country so much they end up wanting to live there permanently.

If a country house is not hemmed in by other buildings it will have around it a free space which can be adapted by the city dweller in the form of a garden or terrace so that he or she feels at home in the country. This is nature tamed, and it can be enhanced if there is enough land and water available to put in a swimming pool.

A swimming pool will add the poetic charm of a pond to the landscape. It is a decorative detail that is always whispering "look at me." Moreover, it is functional.

In any civilization water must not remain the patrimony of a privileged minority. It is only in this century that most of society has been able to enjoy their own interior bathing facilities. Bathing in the sea for medical prescription was the origin of the current summer exodus to the coast.

There are many swimming pools situated on the edge of a precipice that play with the visual effect of a water plane silhouetted cleanly against the horizon. This pool uses the two levels so that the water overflows into a circular fountain below, thereby creating an artificial cascade. It is roughly a fall of six feet and constitutes a decorative, therapeutic artifact. You can stroll down to the second level via a soft grass slope that leads to some steps.

The walls that hold back the earth by the slope, and the water, start from the circular pool. A protected area has been produced where straight and curved planes have been combined. As a general rule, this model is used when the swimming pool must be situated near the limits of the land, in this case the outer wall. On the grass around the pool, bushes, rocks, and flower beds have been introduced. As no area of the garden is paved, the landscape's wild, rustic character is reinforced.

On the grass around the pool
bushes, rocks, and flower
beds have been introduced.

A simple garden

Monaco

The space around the pool is organized symmetrically.

The scent of resin and pine needles transports us to summer in a Mediterranean forest. Days of intense heat and high humidity commence in early July and continue on until September.

The image in the photo could be what many vacationers on the French coast see when they get up every morning—the promise of tranquillity and fun. The swimming pool is in the foreground, the pines and the sea in the background. When we were children, summer officially began with a trip down to the beach, either sandy or rocky, depending on the coastal zone. The path was often overgrown with thorns or rocks that wobbled when we stood on them, or it could be steep. The bushes could snag in our sun-tanned legs, leaving little white marks.

On our return to the house after a dip in the sea, a dive into the pool got rid of the salt and sand. And the day had not finished: There was still the setting of the sun, slipping gently over the horizon. From the terrace, the spectacular views are accompanied by the quiet rustle of the forest.

Obviously, for this type of summer garden, the swimming pool is a key factor. It is not a question of mixing forms, but rather of relating the elements so that the final result is all-inclusive and daring. The lawn that surrounds the pool is lined by trees that serve as a visual dividing line that isolates the space, making it more intimate. The way people live in a summer house, or retreat, is radically different from their urban lifestyle.

The design for the free space has yet to be resolved. While architectural styles can change, the landscape is constant—a necessary complement. Outside, the house is surrounded by greenery: The Mediterranean landscape demands that the lay of the land and the architecture play a role.

An intense blue sea is visible
behind the trunks of the pine trees.

Visual continuity

Menorca. Spain

Next to this swimming pool there is a small circular vantage point. You can sit on the swimming pool wall while you look out.

When a home builder has a sloping plot overlooking the sea, the temptation to create a visually continuous plane with the pool surface and the ocean is, apparently, irresistible.

Given this tendency, the most sophisticated design is to conceal the rim of the pool nearest to the sea, which requires that the water be collected below, thereby obtaining a perfect visual union between the two water planes.

Without doubt, the effect is spectacular. However, there are important conditions if the project is going to be a success. First, this option dictates that the swimming pool be located in the garden, forcing it to be in one of its limits. Second, only one side can be used for entering the pool. Third, an area behind the cascade wall that is difficult to put to good use is produced. Summing up, it is a landscape option that gives splendid visual results but has practical drawbacks.

It is also worth pointing out that according to the Chinese millenium tradition of feng-shui, the best way to situate a house is with a mountain behind and the water in front. However, the water must not be stagnant but moving. Besides heeding the Chinese, there are other reasons why it is wise to clean and change the pool water regularly.

If we swim toward the pool edge at the top of the drop there is nothing that blocks our view. The Mediterranean Sea stretches out before us, lapping against the harsh coast. The coastline is formed by little coves, often hidden, which are difficult to access. The wide-open sandy beaches are further to the south. As the rocks go right down to the water level, the pine trees grow near the water and it is typical to see the ocean blue behind their branches.

On one side of the pool there is a semicircular vantage point over the treetops. These rotundas are found on many of the paths, or tracks, that lead from one coastal town to the next, or from one fortress to the following. These continuous

comings and goings were aimed at ensuring that no unknown boat could steal up on anyone and to facilitate sounding a warning. In some places these paths become even more winding and are literally ledges on the precipice. Now that there are railings, strolling along these paths is a pleasant outing. The seascape is stunning.

The water plane extends as far as the confines of the garden.

Less is more

Architect: Bet Figueras and Maria Jover
Barcelona. Spain

A swimming pool is an open space from which to behold the rest of the environment. It is a special place for making contact with nature and gazing at the horizon. A swimming pool may be a long horizontal sculpture that has to complement the house.

We are on a hillside in the mountains that surround Barcelona to the north. A clearing in front of a house has been turned into a garden amid the pines and low forest.

Constructing a landscape is exactly the opposite of treating nature as a passive element. It means working on a space with a project design that is deliberately seeking a specific look. The person who builds a landscape uses the topographic elements available to him or her, the plant species at hand, and the views. Everything can enter the game as is deemed necessary.

Changing the landscape also means including time as a factor in the project because the worked materials change with the seasons, with the temperature, and with day and night. Seasonal change is important to landscape architecture because it involves the spectator in the process of experiencing the project. Nothing remains unchanged for long and it is the onlooker who will notice the variations that take place.

The swimming pool level is accessed by climbing some stairs on one side of the house. A gently sloping lawn leads down to a gangway that rims an edge of the pool. At one end it widens to form an open-air "living room," with armchairs and a table beneath a pillared wooden roof. All the points of this pool are suitable for staring at the city as it runs to the sea. Through the day it changes—its pace, the light, the buzz of everyday activities—for in some ways it is alive.

Where the interior of the water is lit at night, the pool is converted into a plane of light. Torchlights spread around the garden complement this effect.

The rest areas have been
designed carefully. The lines are
pure and the elements minimal.

Horizontality dominates the lines of the project.

A well-deserved rest

Architect: Josep Joan Pere + Antoni Puig
GCA Arquitectes Associats
Alella. Spain

It is difficult to determine if the house is the form nearest to us in our environment, our most personal territory, or whether it is simply an extension of ourselves, a second skin. On one hand any house belongs to the landscape and is influenced by the topography, by its orientation, and by light and sun. Weather and erosion affect it. However, at the same time, the house is defined by what we do in it, by our activities. Every space has meaning when we do something in it: when we work, rest, and eat. This is why it can be considered an extension of ourselves. Halfway between what we feel is our own and what is not totally ours, a house constitutes an element of culture and of language.

The design of a house enables us to interpret the tastes, character, and image that the owner wants to project. In this case the purity of the lines stands out, both in the house itself and in the layout of the garden and swimming pool. Using minimal construction elements and few materials, a perfect integration of the artificial elements into the landscape has been achieved. There is a note of abstraction in the architectural and natural forms.

When art or design is restrained, when the forms are simple, when everything that is superfluous has been reduced as much as possible, we say that it is minimalist. In architecture, when we speak of minimalism, it is clear that there exists a tradition of geometric rigor, formal constraint, and conceptual purism to which it is indebted. Rationalism prepared the way, but the intentions and concerns of today's architects are different.

This dwelling seeks the protection of the hillside and the trees on the north face, while it is open to the views of the plain, where the swimming pool is located.

On the north side, the
house is sheltered by the
mountain, while still
offering fine sea views.

The thickness of the Mediterranean pine and low bush forest contrasts with the
spacious clearing in front of the house from where we can contemplate the horizon,
the sea, and the edge of the pool-water plane. The palette of blues and greens is
enriched according to the time of day and the different seasons, ranging through a
multitude of hues.

The flooring of long wooden strips, combined with a grass lawn, surrounds the
swimming pool. On the warm wooden floor some state-of-the-art reclining deck
chairs have been placed for us to gaze at the sea. This relaxation area is marked off
with flower beds in which plants have been groomed into geometric shapes.

A swimming pool with a view

Toulon. France

This is a swimming pool of simple, restrained, and precise lines. The ornaments have been reduced to the minimum, and it appears to be an embodiment of the slogan "more is less," which is so pervasive in modern architecture. This simplicity pays off when the environment itself is alluring. Thus the architecture does not seek to compete with the landscape, but rather to be a frame for it, or a place from which it can be contemplated. In some ways it appears like an empty stage upon which the choreography of the vacation will be enacted. A great white wall rises up on one side of the swimming pool like a stage backdrop, complementing the space and flooding the atmosphere with a diffused light reflected from the blue ripples on the water.

The water remains calm, like an impenetrable mirror that duplicates the tops of the pine trees, creating a fantastic world of trunkless trees.

One of the main reasons why the decision to construct the swimming pool on this spot was made was to take advantage of the wonderful views, enabling sunbathers to see how the forest slopes gently down to the sea. A language of subtle gestures and soothing colors creates a silence in the midst of the vernal murmuring of the forest and a place to rest your eyes.

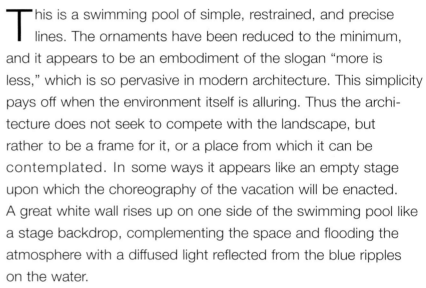

The protagonism of the swimming pool means that it is not only a leisure space for the summer; it is also a permanent reference for the whole house throughout the year.

The laws of composition that are applied to these few elements—swimming pool, wall, pavement, and handrail—come from considerations closely linked to minimalist art. Foremost in importance are the scale relationships, the texture of the materials, and the way the light falls on the objects. One could be fooled into the impression that this type of architecture isolates us from the sensuality of nature. However, the landscape is out there, making iits presence felt with the change of seasons, the wind that rustles the leaves, the dry periods, the wet months, all of which adds up to give us the perception that time is the continuous repetition of cycles.

Perhaps this is the most important achievement of one type of architecture: the realization that it is not enough just to provide shelter. In addition, it is necessary for the appearance of a structure to constantly give us clues about what we are like and what our role in the world is.

A water canal

Architect: José Antonio Martínez Lapeña
and Elias Torres Tur
Ibiza. Spain

The architecture is staggered to imitate the slope of the Mediterranean forest.

A swimming pool situated on sloping ground has to be thought out very differently from those on flat ground. The construction must take into consideration that it will support the weight of the water. Although it can be more expensive, this swimming pool opens up a lot of possibilities in terms of views and stands out more against the landscape.

In this swimming pool the bathing area has been separated from the swimming area. Parallel to the slope a long canal that enables us to play sports without disturbing the tranquillity of the other bathers has been dug.

The residence is located half a level above the water plane and is accessed via some stairs that resemble the steps of a classic plinth. While the bathing area enjoys a fine panorama over the Mediterranean forest, the entrance is partially shielded by the wall, protecting the intimacy of the house. The patio-terrace is typical of traditional architecture in this area, and is justified not only by social convention but also by climatic considerations. The patio, normally in the center of the house, is a shady space that regulates the temperature in the home. The rooms open onto this controlled area, letting in cooler, fresher air. Plants, trees, and creepers are cultivated, and chairs and tables are laid out for summer meals.

In this case the patio has been located in the entrance, as a transition space between inside and outside, so that it acts as a filter and as a terrace that links us with the landscape. Beyond this controlled area, the fragile pines shed needles until they form a carpet. For the forest to be accessible it is important to get rid of the weeds, shrubs, and undergrowth, and to prune the lower branches of the trees. This will offer better views as well as prevent any fire spreading rapidly.

The swimming pool, too, is organized to make it as comfortable as possible. Besides the separation between bathing and swimming already mentioned, there is a wooden platform where we can sunbathe. The double function of many areas makes the whole setup more flexible: It can be used in many ways, according to the imagination.

The swimming pool is divided
into two areas, one for relaxing
and the other for swimming.

173

TROPICAL SWIMMING POOLS

In this group of pools we will find those that are in the tropical region or a nearby latitude. They have in common the climate, which is characterized by intense rainstorms and the harsh sun. The vegetation is normally lush and fast growing. This makes for a unique natural environment graced by a great variety of plant species, a warm climate, and the beauty of its coastlines, some of which are abrupt and some soft and white. As the temperature is high year-round it is possible to lead an outdoor life, enjoying nature without any filters. The swimming pools that are set out before us are perfectly integrated into this dream landscape and fit in with the image that we have of idyllic vacations, which are now more attainable than ever. The pools are located in Puerto Vallarta in Mexico, Guanica in Puerto Rico, La Romana and La Península de Samana in the Dominican Republic, Lankawy in Malaysia, Java and Lombok in Indonesia, and Malibu in the United States.

Backlight

Puerto Vallarta. Mexico

When the sun sets there is a strong backlight that silhouettes the different components of this imaginative design.

Everyone of us at some time has wanted to escape from his or her daily routine, leave it all behind, and walk into a world of blue seas and palm trees. This image, which naturally comes to mind with tropical landscapes, forms part of the collective imagination. However, although tourism has made these dream landscapes accessible to so many of us, our fascination with them has not waned. Changing anything or building on these idyllic locations is a delicate operation. The architecture must fit in with the local tradition and landscape.

There are two ways of conceptualizing a pool: Project it from the hollow shape, "in negative," or start out considering the solid shapes: the pool full of water, "in positive." You have to decide if it is the ground that determines the form, or if it is the swimming pool that gives shape to its surroundings.

In this case we can clearly see that the architect has started out from a large space in negative. The pool is treated like a mold that has been filled with water and then later adorned here and there with new solid elements of different shapes: islands connected by bridges, palm trees, tables, lounge chairs, and umbrellas made out of branches.

This approach has enriched the project because it is possible to access it from different directions. The water flow and the architectural flow sometimes cross paths, slowing down, accelerating, complementing, and contrasting with each other.

The landscape offers us very heterogenous elements. There are parterres, flowerpots, pavements, and even half-finished arches cut back as if the passage of time had interrupted the work so that they remained unfinished, suspended in the air.

When the sun sets there is a strong backlight that silhouettes and darkens the outline of this imposing architecture. The light is reflected by the water, while the shadows become denser and more still as, little by little, they blanket the ground.

Within this large swimming pool, which is spread over the ground like a lake, a curious visual effect is created: Like a *trompe l'oeil*, it plays with the eye of the beholder. In one area the edge of the water disappears and the swimming pool is superimposed on top of the ocean as if it were a more luminous plane. Along the line of intersection there appears fungilike boxwood umbrellas in little groups, lest we forget that below there is a stretch of beach.

Far away a white hulk suddenly breaks the horizon. It is another transatlantic liner arriving at the coast, bringing home the reality that this landscape does not belong solely to us: We are purely admirers of its beauty and soon we will have to leave. We are just passersby.

A tradition of comfort

Malibu. California. USA

The use of water has spiritual and practical connotations for it offers a sense of infinity, like being in the country in front of an open space. Here a swimming pool has been built together with a pavilion to hold back the lush greenery.

On the clear bottom of the swimming pool a mosaic pattern depicts three dolphins—a motif reminding us that the sea is near.

The pavilion is decorated with geometric and floral motifs. Inside there are benches and a table. The coolness of this shady area is welcome. Our eyes can relax from squinting in the strong light reflected by the still water.

The abundant rainfall of most coastal and tropical areas has made water a key part of life and specifically of gardens, sometimes as a result of destiny, sometimes as a response to the need to control it and collect it, and sometimes as a complement to the natural lushness of the vegetation and flowers.

Projects based on the plenitude of water characterize some of the earliest tropical gardens designed around the first Hindu palaces and Buddhist temples. The water was thrown into the channels and ponds by fountains that were decorated with deities and grotesque animals. Frequently the water was closely related to the buildings, sometimes in an artistic way, but often as a solution to a practical problem, as was the case with the Buddhist monasteries in Thailand, where the libraries were set up in small pavilions over a canal or a lake to protect the manuscripts from the white ants. The strong European influences that were assimilated by many tropical countries during the long period of colonial and commercial domination were what definitively introduced architectural formality into these gardens.

In this project the traditional relationship between formal and natural elements is characterized by the playoff between textures, colors, and sounds. The exuberance, variety, and hardiness of the greenery combine to form a composition in which water is always indispensable.

The tradition of the gardens in Asia always has been based on an art intimately related to philosophy and religion, landscape paintings, and poetry. These gardens have a significance that transcends their appearance. Water and mountains are two elements that most often have been used symbolically, commonly represented by water running over rocks.

This project aims at reproducing an ideal landscape, be it natural or artificial, in which these two contrasting elements fit: feminine and masculine, water and rock.

The palm trees introduce a vertical element which contrasts with the breadth of the horizon.

The last afternoon hour

Architect: Sierra, Cardona, Ferrer Arquitectos
Guanica. Puerto Rico

There is a landscape that can transport us to another world where we leave our daily problems behind and just learn to live for the present. The therapeutic power of an image of a beach with palm trees, sea, and sun is huge.

One session a day while seated in front of a slide show of tropical landscapes should be a requirement to reduce the stress and aggression of the average city dweller. If, moreover, we can become part of one of the photos, then we are really onto a good thing.

When the sun beats down hard, moving into the shade is not enough. It is time for us to have a swim and rest on the deck chairs, wondering at the beauty of the virgin natural landscape along the shoreline. At dusk the sinking sun lights up the sky, silhouetting the palm trees against the sky, the blue of which is enhanced by the blue of the ocean as it laps toward the beach. On the horizon the blue is ultramarine, and beyond the coral reef it is turquoise.

When we do not want to go completely out into the wild, but want an equally appetizing bath closer to home, we can slip into a grand pool near the building. Here we can enjoy all the comforts that we are accustomed to in front of an exceptional tropical backdrop. Stretching out before us there is a grass lawn that merges with the tree area and allows us to walk barefoot without scorching our feet.

This natural garden is an ideal place in which to observe the behavior of the different species of wildlife and to enjoy the changing seasons and climates.

There has been no landscape designing here; no frames have been set up. Rather there has been an attempt to control the unrestrained tropical growth.

The psychological importance of nature can be measured when it is not present. The art of organizing the placements, laying out the different buildings in such a blessed landscape, is the architect's responsibility. Some people think that architects have to be landscape supervisors.

In the big cities architects design landscapes. In spite of the existence of artificial parks, these landscapes are necessary oases, lungs that emit clean air. City dwellers live for any opportunity to hide away momentarily from the noise and the pollution. This is why they take advantage of their vacations to get away from the asphalt and take refuge in faroff, virgin locations.

The house blends into the lush garden.

A space to be shared

Architect: Bill Cox
Casa de Campo. La Romana. Dominican Republic

Down on the beach, almost at the sand's edge, we would love to find a small house reminiscent of a wooden boathouse or fishermen's shack, away from the high-rise apartment blocks overrun by shouting children. This would be an ideal place to stay during the holidays to cut ourselves off from every reminder of civilization. Architecture, up until now, has applied the same formula to beautiful landscapes as to cities, and has thus ended up destroying them.

Fortunately, after years of excesses, which sometimes damaged the landscape irreversibly, there has emerged a new concept of architecture that respects the natural environment and tries to blend the piece harmoniously into the scenery. To achieve this end it is necessary to follow a series of rules about materials, finishings, volume, heights, and color.

In this project three bungalow apartments have been joined together in a U shape that goes around a gangway that accesses all of them. This wooden gangway is wide enough to be used as a terrace from which to look over the swimming pool, which is situated in the center. One of the eaves of the double-sloped roof covers the gangway, converting it into a porch.

This type of construction brings to mind the typical interstate roadside motels in the United States. The bungalows, too, have a common entrance and the dwellings are along one side.

The swimming pool is for everyone in the community and is big enough to swim some serious lengths. Around the pool, irregularly sized rock slabs invite you to get the lounge chairs out to soak up the sun. Behind the houses the tropical greenery closes in, even brushing against the roofs with its bendy branches, camouflaging the architecture. In front of the site there is a garden of low vegetation dotted with palm trees, and at the bottom are the sea, the horizon, and the sky.

In the central part of the shared patio an astutely placed table enables us to sit down and have a drink while relaxing our eyes with the view, or to dine under the moon and candlelight contemplating the night landscape.

In the climates that afford outdoor life, it is very important to understand how to design shared spaces. Where they are situated has to be carefully considered, as does their relationship with the private area. It is wise that they be not too mixed and able to be separated when necessary.

An idyllic landscape

Design: Natasha Despotovic
Las Galeras. Samana's Peninsula.
Dominican Republic

The architecture of the path and the stairs tends to be symmetric, contrasting with the randomness of the landscape.

The presence of a beach transforms the architecture. The beach calls into existence a sensual, playful, often disconcerting world, converting the architecture into a direct, no-holds-barred, and spontaneous creation.

The constructions near the beach reveal how changeable, ephemeral, and random everything can be. They manifest the intense sensation of movement and provisionality that impregnates the landscape in the same way that the untidy proliferation of mobile elements is symbolic of the absence of anything permanent.

Often beachfront land is turned into an eyesore of huge advertising signs. It can be spoiled by oversized billboards that reflect the fantasies of consumer society. There are terraces like boat decks and palm trees that create little Malibus. These images of today's culture give the ambience an unreal, playful feeling.

In this case, beyond the physical reality, the landscape has a mythical quality. It is a place that is immediately recognizable, for we have seen it before somewhere else. It is not just a plot of land; this landscape is full of evocative connotations of exotic adventurous lives. An underlying and unifying image of tranquillity, of leisure, of full and direct contact with nature is added to the topography, to the vegetation, and to the careful setting of every object.

The architecture is light and transparent. The white painted wood adds a warm, happy touch. The wide openings in the walls let the light penetrate inside, revealing everything. If we softly descend the stairs and follow the path through the low vegetation we will come to a small bridge from which we can make out the sinuous swimming pool and the beach line marked by rocks. The wind relentlessly rustles the palm trees, and the noise of the leaves is added to that of the waves breaking on the shore, near the rocks.

In the foreground, a hammock hung from the porch sways gently in the wind. Lying in it, in the shade, we can savor the beauty of the landscape.

The swimming pool seems to be a cavity in the landscape, a perforation in the rocky relief that has been filled with water by the last rains. Its softly curved form is integrated perfectly into the environment. The white rim stands out against the vegetation like the sand contrasted against the palm trees.

Natural scenery

Designer: Bibí León
Casa de Campo. La Romana
Dominican Republic

At one end of the swimming pool a pavilion has been built. It is a simple shed supported by pillars.

Near the tropics the climate always varies in the same way throughout the day. The sky is a changing backdrop crossed by high, very white clouds. It is only clear for a few hours; normally the sun is partially filtered.

This natural scenery has so much strength that it does not need decorating. What is necessary is to clear the terrain that the swimming pool is going to occupy, build it, put flooring around it, and perhaps construct a pavilion that offers shade. This minimalist structure is adequate enough to provide an area in which to settle down and enjoy the landscape. In the depths of our subconscious we remember that these islands could have been paradise, with flora and fauna that seem to have been lifted from our most exotic fantasies: lands where all our dreams are possible.

When we visit this paradise after a busy work week, we can stay in the hotel, or in the beach apartments, or in the bungalows, which afford a better integration of the architecture and the landscape. Few people have a private residence in these spots, only the privileged.

At one end of the swimming pool, on top of some pillars, there is a small construction with a tiled roof reminiscent of ancient dwellings, the first shelters to protect humans from the weather. Normally these shelters were constructed with palm branches woven together, forming various layers that made them impermeable to the rain. Such simplicity adds a personal touch. There is ample room for chairs and tables so that we can relax in the shade. This shed is as wide as the swimming pool. It fills up one end and gives it an elevation. In this way the space that surrounds the bathing area is more intimate and is not lost in the far horizon.

A second lawn runs down to the first line of palm trees. The hard pavement that surrounds the swimming pool softens as it touches live vegetation. Between these two pavements there are modern citylike lanterns that denote man's domain.

The swimming pool is on an
esplanade of different pavements.

Luxury and comfort

Java. Indonesia

The reflection is the other side of the world. It appears when the surface of the water is completely still, as if it were a mirror. The images thrown back fade away when a gentle breeze picks up and makes little ripples that softly contort the image. This spectacular world is as fragile as a glass pane and as ephemeral as a calm day.

To bring this reflection close to the house it is necessary only to build a swimming pool with its tame waters nearby. This enormous swimming pool fills the entire area with vibrant light. It has an irregular profile, marking out terraced areas for resting, and is surrounded by palm trees.

The landscape transports us to a realm where dreams become reality and life takes us through a movie screen into an adventure film in a far-off and exotic land. This is a space in which it is possible to meditate and contemplate the views, while at the same time enjoying a glamorous and luxurious social life. The openness of the panorama contrasts with the overcrowding that we endure in the city. Here, solitude is possible, but it is a solitude that is sought after, positive, and worthwhile.

Doing physical exercise in this expansive landscape is another delight of this vacation world. One can swim in the tranquil waters of the swimming pool or contemplate the blue depths of the nearby coral reef, go water skiing, or simply ramble across the land.

A European style combines with the indigenous style to create an architecture full of charm that blends with the landscape. Western culture supplies the luxury and the comfort while local tradition dictates that the building be somewhat lightweight, transparent, and very warm. The natural materials take the architecture closer to the people, making them feel the constant presence of nature directly.

The views from underneath the pergola, like in a splendid garden, make it a pleasant place to chat while looking out over the sea. A straw umbrella will also provide shelter from any late-afternoon shower that may fall.

This is the world of outdoor living, of relaxation, and of getting away from stress, where everyday problems can be forgotten and we can learn to value things differently. This peace gives us an inner strength.

After passing through a shadowy area, we come to the open space of the swimming pool. The architectural lines compose an image dominated by the symmetry.

A light spot

Lankawy. Malaysia

Knowing when to play the trump card is very important when planning a garden. Here it has been done astutely. Before us we have an unconventional design that instead of placing the swimming pool in an intimate corner puts it in the center of the axis upon which all eyes fall. The pool provokes curious glances that try to discover what is hidden behind this wooden gangway, and where it leads.

In Asian gardens the idea of a path we travel down always has some meaning. It is never a random or fortuitous progression. It is a route taking us from one place to another that will certainly have different characteristics. A course that follows a winding path is very distinct from one that is direct. With the former we discover the landscape gradually; every curve will reveal something new to us. The rhythm is unhurried and melodious. With a straight line the objective is to get there, to go through something, or to pass over it, but, above all, to reach the other side.

The building is laid out in terraces and when seen from below gives off an image of sturdiness due to the robust walls formed by the different levels. Almost as a contrast to this open and luminous part of the garden, the whole area behind the pavilion has been turned into a shady area, sheltered from the sun by the thick and lush indigenous vegetation. The architectual lines compose an image dominated by a symmetry broken only by elements of the landscape. Indeed, the landscape is a perfect complement to the architecture, with its chaotic framework of trunks, bushes, plants, and flowers through which the light filters with difficulty. In this context, the swimming pool stands out like a mirror under the open sky, reflecting the surroundings.

The pavilion next to the swimming pool is raised on a small plinth and is formed with a straw roof in compliance with the local building customs. Its geometry is very characteristic of the area. As the rains can be heavy, the roof must be quite steep.

The philosophy behind this design is based on the belief that a residence must reflect the tradition of a place, the needs and the personalities of its owners. One of the concerns of the project was to make sure that the spaces were sufficiently isolated from each other to ensure as much privacy as possible, while at the same time maintaining direct contact with the garden and natural light. This means that the close relationship with nature—the change of

seasons, the varying light, the trees, the shades of the colors, the blossoming of the flowers, and the fruits is preserved.

The architecture has to enable us to feel all these transformations in a silent and intimate environment that enables us to be contemplative.

One's own territory

Lombok. Indonesia

Besides marking off the limits of the private property, the architectural barriers that surround the gardens and swimming pool have the function of protecting the people from the jungle.

In Asian tradition water has always been used artfully and intelligently. Thermals, baths, spas, and gardens were designed with exquisite care and special symbolism. Due to its abundance it is an element of the landscape that is as important as the vegetation. In places where exuberant greenery ends up invading everything, one has to be constantly fighting to conserve a habitable space. This is why the ground must be paved, walls to hold back the trees erected, slopes staggered, and the soil retained.

Once we have managed to tame a portion of the land, the pleasure of enjoying the landscape and the climate knows no limits. The large swimming pool that presides over the living quarters is for rest and recreation. Its waters reflect the intense tropical light. The discomfort that bothers us all day long disappears after a dip and a cool siesta in one of the comfortable deck chairs around the swimming pool. Fortunately, some umbrellas will protect us from the harsh rays if we fall into a profound slumber.

The tapestry means that from this angle we can see the domelike roofs of the outbuildings standing out against the palm trees in the background.

The different types of architecture form a new pattern, playing with the ambience and making nature more human. The attractiveness of the landscape, although it is full of magical meaning, comes from the human intervention, from the fusion of the wild backdrop and the modified aspects. It is like a blank canvas on top of which we draw by spreading out different textures and transparencies.

Beyond the swimming pool we can find some pleasant corners with benches, tables, and wooden chairs to eat in when dusk falls, or simply to have a softdrink while conversing.

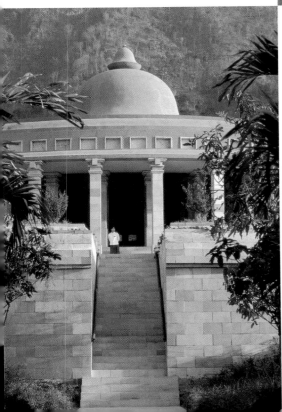

A wooden banister signals the level change. This whole area is like a boat jetty on the coast, with the noise of the water beating at our feet as we bask in the beautiful view over the majestic ocean.

Blending in with the landscape

Architect: Roberto Cappa
Casa de Campo. La Romana. Dominican Republic

Situated among palm trees, surrounded by lush tropical vegetation, this house has been constructed on a wooden platform that runs like a terrace, incorporating the trees into the domestic landscape. The palm trees emerge out of the pavement as if they were part of the garden. The swimming pool, which is in the middle of them, adapts its shape so as not to swallow them up.

The nearness of the trees does not hinder the maintenance of the water because their leaves do not fall off easily. Moreover, given their great height, thinness, and relatively small crown, they do not cast a very thick shadow: They are only a first filter of solar radiation. The movement of the trunks and branches creates a colorful, variegated light pattern.

The roofing of the house runs beyond the walls and helps to create a shady area in which to sit tranquilly and contemplate the swimming pool with the sea behind. Against one wall of the porch is a bench with large screen-printed back cushions that add an Asian air to this transition space between the house and the intense daylight.

Although the climate seems idyllic and tranquil, in a few moments it can rage up into a storm. These areas, depending on the season, are liable to suffer from the scourge of hurricanes, cyclones, and tornados. These meteorological phenomena are unpredictable and often have devastating effects. Therefore, the architecture must take this risk into account: It must be flexible and perfectly adapted to the ground as well as offer protection from the harsh sunrays. Extended eaves reaching out provide shade. The construction materials chosen must be able to withstand the humidity and the salinity of the atmosphere.

On one side of the porch, at the swimming pool level, there is a breakfast table. Plates and glasses have been laid out ready for the early risers who wish to start the day with a dose of energy.

From this sheltered corner, a little higher than sand level, we can look down on the intricate panorama of palm tree trunks that before our eyes paint an abstract canvas of lines and color stains. In some places the sea reaches into little inlets, producing an unexpected splash and sparkle of water.